GETTING DOWN TO
BRASS
TACKS

Advice from James for Real-World Christians

O.S. HAWKINS

Getting Down to Brass Tacks
©1993 by O. S. Hawkins
Revised 2010

Library of Congress Cataloging-in-Publication Data
Hawkins, O. S.
Getting Down to Brass Tacks / O.S. Hawkins.
Includes bibliographical references.
ISBN 978-097794003-5
1. Bible. N.T. James-Commentaries. I. Title.
BS2785.3.H39 1992
227.9107-dc2O   92-17821

2010926726

Printed in the United States of America.
10 9 8 7 6 5 4 3 2 1

GuideStone·
Financial Resources

❀ OTHER BOOKS BY O.S. HAWKINS ❀

When Revival Comes
After Revival Comes
Clues to a Successful Life
Where Angels Fear to Tread
Tracing the Rainbow Through the Rain
Revive Us Again
Unmasked!
Jonah: Meeting the God of the Second Chance
Getting Down to Brass Tacks
In Sheep's Clothing
Tearing Down Walls and Building Bridges
Moral Earthquakes and Secret Faults
Rebuilding: It's Never Too Late for a New Beginning
Money Talks: But What Is It Really Saying?
Shields of Brass or Shields of Gold?
Good News for Great Days
Drawing the Net
Culture Shock
High Calling, High Anxiety
The Question of Our Time
The Art of Connecting
GuideStones: Ancient Landmarks
The Pastor's Primer
More Good News for Great Days

⊛ DEDICATION ⊛

To Jackson Hawkins Shivers

Our first grandchild of whom I say what Paul

once said of one of his own sons in the faith,

"He is my own heart."

You will always bear my name and

take with you my heart and prayers all your days.

I am very proud to be your grandfather.

TABLE OF CONTENTS

⊛ FOREWORD ⊛

There could be no more fascinating or pertinent message to humanity than that from James, the blood brother of the Lord Jesus Christ, the younger son of Joseph and Mary of Nazareth. To look at the world and its physical and spiritual life through the eyes of a man of God like James is a breathtaking opportunity. His letter is possibly the first piece of New Testament literature that has been presented to us. His position as pastor of the church at Jerusalem commands our immediate and continuing attention. To hear and read what James has to say about the Christian faith is an open door into the light of Heaven.

Who is equipped to expound this practical letter of James, the undershepherd of the first church at Jerusalem? No one is more qualified to interpret, through pastoral experience and Christian leadership, the admonitions of this first-century Christian than Dr. O.S. Hawkins. Through years of ministry, he has come to realize the spiritual depths and practicalities of this letter from the pen of James.

To know Dr. O.S. Hawkins is to be introduced to a "people person" and a shepherd of the flock whose life is enmeshed in that of his church. James, too, knew all about the problems and trials of his congregation. He knew the blessings and the triumphs that could await their victories in the Lord Jesus. Whether it was in prayer or ministering to the poor, James lived the life of his people and by inspiration brought to them God's answers to all the providences faced in their pilgrim journey. These words and characterizations of the life and ministry of Pastor James are also true of Pastor Hawkins. Read James and you are introduced to the heights and depths of the Christian faith. Read this book by Pastor Hawkins and you will follow in the same marvelous pilgrim way.

You who hold this book in your hands are fortunate. You whose eyes look upon this Scriptural exposition are blessed of God. You will have achieved a marvelous milestone in your Christian understanding when you incarnate these Christian principles into your daily walk with Christ. May God wonderfully bless you as you read this extraordinarily faithful exposition of one of the truly great portions of God's infallible Word.

W. A. Criswell
(Foreword to first edition 1993)

❈ INTRODUCTION ❈

"Getting down to brass tacks." This well-worn phrase finds its origin in the old-fashioned fabric stores. When a customer would decide on a certain type and color of cloth, the shopkeeper would put the roll of fabric on his counter and stretch it out. Brass tacks were imbedded along the edge of the counter in one-foot intervals. The shopkeeper would measure the amount of cloth requested by counting the brass tacks along the counter. Thus, when a customer had made her selection and was ready to make her purchase, she would often say to the clerk, "Let's get down to brass tacks." And so the phrase has found its way into our vocabulary and onto the cover of this volume since the contents describe what it means to get down to the real business at hand, to get down to details and do something about it.

Getting down to brass tacks means getting down to the bottom line, trimming away all the excess and the nonessentials, coming straight to the point and getting down to the basics. This is the burden of James' letter to those scattered in the first-century diaspora, and to those of us who now live in the third millennium. In a unique and challenging way, the letter brings all of us face to face with the importance in our Christian walk of... GETTING DOWN TO BRASS TACKS!

The book of James is the most practical New Testament epistle. Even as the church now ministers to a world 2,000 years removed from its writing, his letter remains as relevant today as our morning newspaper. Why? Because the 13 themes that James addressed are timeless. He called upon us not simply to hear the word of God, but to "do it." In the words of a popular athletic shoe advertisement, James said, "JUST DO IT!"

What is the first thing we do when we receive a letter? Most of us look at the bottom of the page to see who signed it before we read it. In ancient days, the author would sign his name at the top. Thus, we read in James 1:1, "James, a servant of God and of the Lord Jesus Christ." The author of this letter is James, the half brother of our Lord Jesus Christ.

Mary and Joseph had several children (Matthew 12:46–48; Mark 6:3). Although James and the other brothers of our Lord did not believe in Christ during His earthly ministry (John 7:1–5), we know that sometime after the resurrection Jesus appeared to James and he became a believer. Paul related that Christ "appeared to James, then to all the apostles" (1 Corinthians 15:7).

James grew to such stature in the faith that he became the undisputed leader of the Jerusalem church and the moderator of the great Jerusalem council (Acts 15). Paul referred to him as a pillar of the church (Galatians 2:9). Tradition tells us that James was a tremendous man of prayer and was often referred to as "camel knees" because of the calluses he earned by spending hour upon hour on his knees in prayer.

Because of his rich heritage, we might have expected the author to begin his letter by saying, "James, leader of the church in Jerusalem" or "James, an apostle of the Lord" or "James, half brother of the Lord Jesus Christ." But he simply referred to himself as "James, a servant." In describing himself as such, he chose to use the Greek word δοῦλος.

A δοῦλος was a slave who had completed his term of service and could have been set free from his master's control. However, after considering everything in the world and all its opportunities, the slave had concluded that he was better off with his master and became a bondslave, a δοῦλος, by choice. He chose the one who first chose him. His earlobe was placed against a doorpost and pierced to signify his new standing. The mark is called in the Greek, "στιγματα." This word was used by Paul in Galatians 6:17 when he said, "I bear on my body the marks [stigmata] of Jesus."

When people saw the δοῦλος walking down the street, they would note the mark on his ear and exclaim, "What a wonderful master he must have. He could have gone free, but he has chosen to stay with his master."

James referred to himself as a δοῦλος, a bondslave. James regarded himself as a servant, a slave of the Lord Jesus Christ. Having been bought with a price, he could never say no to his Master.

One distinguishing characteristic of a great man is that he does not think that he is great. Someone said, "The great man never thinks he is great, and the small man never thinks he is small." My pastor used to tell me that if I thought I was too big for a little job, then I was too little for a big job. The secret of success in the Christian life is for each of us to find our position as a δοῦλος. Our Lord said that the greatest of all men born of women was John the Baptist, and John the Baptist said, "He must become greater; I must become less" (John 3:30).

James addressed his letter "to the twelve tribes scattered among the nations" (James 1:1). In the language of the New Testament the word for "scattered" is διασπορά. From it, we get the English words dispersed and dispersion. Those who were dispersed were scattered like seed. After Stephen was killed outside the Lions Gate of the city of Jerusalem, Christians were scattered [diaspora] throughout the Roman world (Acts 8:1–3).

God permitted this test of the Jerusalem church for a purpose. Had there been no diaspora, the Christians might well have stayed in Jerusalem and the growth of the church would have been stymied. Instead, in one generation the gospel was spread throughout the known world — all the way to the confines of Rome itself.

James wrote his letter to Christian Jews scattered outside Palestine. He wrote to those who had been dispersed, to those who had to leave their homes, their jobs and their property. However, he was writing to us too, because in one sense all

Christians are in the diaspora. We are living as exiles from our eternal heavenly home. Thus, the letter of James is directly from God to us, for behind the hand of James is the hand of God. "All Scripture is God-breathed and is useful for teaching, rebuking, correcting and training in righteousness" (2 Timothy 3:16).

James wrote his letter to those under persecution in order to teach them how to deal with the stress and pressure of difficult trials. He was writing to women who were at their wit's end. Their children were screaming and crying, and trying to adjust to new surroundings. He was writing to men who had lost their jobs and their sense of dignity. The people who would read his letter were literally hanging by a thread. Persecution had driven them from their homes. They were wrestling with how to live out what they believed. Consequently, James was extremely practical and even at times polemic. Christians today also face pressure and stress. We, too, can learn from James how to react.

The book of James is the most practical letter in the New Testament. The burden of his message is that we should become "doers of the word, and not hearers only" (James 1:22 KJV). James was more of a "hands-on" practitioner than a theologian. He got his hands dirty. He called upon the church in any age to practice what it preaches. He challenged us to come face to face with the need of...GETTING DOWN TO BRASS TACKS!

⊛ CHAPTER ONE ⊛

STRESS: FIVE FASCINATING FACTS
JAMES 1:1–12

I. Stress Is Predictable (James 1:1–2)
II. Stress Is Problematic (James 1:2)
III. Stress Is Paradoxical (James 1:2–4)
IV. Stress Is Purposeful (James 1:3–8)
V. Stress Is Profitable (James 1:9–12)

S-T-R-E-S-S has become the buzzword of our generation. The dictionary defines stress as "pressure...intense strain... to bind tight...to subject to external forces." People finger stress as the blasting cap that activates such problems as heart trouble, hypertension, cancer, headaches, relational strains, divorces and hundreds of other difficulties. Stress is the scapegoat, the excuse of modern man.

The moment we hear the word "stress," many of us clench our fists and tighten up as if stress were our foe. The truth is, "stress" is not a four-letter word and can be our friend. Stress can be one of life's greatest assets when we learn to handle it properly. Stress can actually lead to longer, happier, healthier and more productive lives when we learn its purpose and begin to control it rather than letting it control us.

One of the greatest secrets of success is to learn how to react under pressure and stress on the job, at home, at school or in the midst of relationships. The book of James teaches us how to live successful, victorious lives.

James wrote his letter to Christians who had been dispersed during the first century. His first words to them were about how to deal with stress and pressure. The recipients of his letter were facing very difficult trials. Therefore James sought to show them, and us, that stress is not necessarily a foe, but can be a friend.

James began his letter by pointing to five fascinating facts that can turn stress from foe to friend. He wanted us to know that stress is predictable, problematic, paradoxical, purposeful and can be profitable.

1. Stress Is Predictable
James 1:1–2

James 1:2 says, "Consider it pure joy, my brothers, whenever you face trials of many kinds." The verse doesn't say "if" we face trials of many kinds; it says "when." The point is, stress is predictable — inevitable, inescapable, unavoidable. We all have it. Some of us have learned to deal with it and some of us haven't. We live in a pressure-packed society and stress is predictable.

In the early '90s, a popular bumper sticker declared, "Stress happens." We often hear the warning, "Avoid stress!" That's impossible, isn't it? Stress is predictable.

We can read the Bible from cover to cover but nowhere will we find a promise that Spirit-filled Christians will be immune to sickness and stress, trials and tribulations. Some people say that if we are living the Spirit-filled life, we will have smooth sailing on the sea of God's will. But Jesus warned, "In this world you will have trouble. But take heart! I have overcome the world" (John 16:33).

Some people never learn to deal with stress because of the erroneous idea that it will go away. In fact, many who have been admonished to avoid stress have simply had more stress heaped upon them — the stress of not knowing how to cope. Yes, stress is inevitable. It is a question of *when*, not *if*.

James said that we should consider it pure joy when we face "trials" of many kinds. "Trials" is a translation of the Greek word πειρασμos. (James wrote his letter in Koine Greek, the universal language of the day.) It can mean either "trials" or "temptations." We have to note the context. Sometimes James used πειρασμός to describe outward trials that are designed to teach Christians to stand firm. In other places, he used the same word to describe inward temptations that cause Christians to stumble. In verse 2, James used it to mean an outward trial or test.

None of us is immune to outward trials that create stress. Interestingly, we never grow out of the possibility of confronting trials. When we study the lives of men and women in the Bible, we find that some of their greatest trials came way down the road of their personal spiritual pilgrimage, not at the beginning of their walk with God.

Consider Moses, for example. After seeing the hand of God in so many wonderful ways — the parting of the Red Sea, the cloud by day and the pillar of fire by night, the manifestation of manna every morning — the complaints of the children of Israel tried his patience. He struck the rock instead of speaking to it, perverting the type of Christ. Think of David — the shepherd, psalmist, king and man after God's own heart. His greatest trials came after he was on the throne of Israel. And what about Simon Peter, the big fisherman? He had proven his courage so many times before, but when confronted on the last evening of Christ's life, he cowered by the fire outside the house of the high priest.

No matter who we are or how long we have walked the journey of the Christian life, we will face stress. The sooner we realize that, the more quickly we will be able to deal with stress. The tragedy of today's tranquilizer mentality is that it simply postpones the day we will eventually have to face the foe.

James said we should consider it pure joy when we "face" trials of many kinds. The word translated "face" in the New International Version and "fall into" in the King James is the Greek περιπίπτω. Found only three times in the entire New Testament, περιπίπτω is the word Jesus used to describe the man on the Jericho road. "A man was going down from Jerusalem to Jericho," He said, "when he *fell into* the hands of robbers" (Luke 10:30, *italics added*). He rounded a corner, and suddenly —WHAM! He was surrounded by unexpected trouble. There was no warning, no time to run away. Trouble sprang upon him. James 1:2 uses the same word to describe how we are sometimes confronted with stressful trials. We sail through life, go around the bend, and WHAM! We "face trials of many kinds."

How many times have we been on this road? Everything is going well and then we get the doctor's report...or the pink slip comes unexpectedly...or death knocks on a loved one's door...or the roof springs a leak...or additional income tax is due.

How should we react? We should begin by realizing that stress is predictable. None of us is immune to it, and none of us can escape it. God is always testing us to make us stronger. Ask Abraham, who God told to sacrifice his only son Isaac. Ask Joseph, who was thrown into an Egyptian dungeon on a trumped-up charge.

Some present-day prophets are propagating a theology that is foreign to the Bible. These "new wave" preachers tell their followers that the cause of sickness or difficulties is sin in their lives or lack of faith. Many gullible and immature Christians fall victim to this false teaching. Then when stressful trials jump upon them, they lose the faith that they thought they had.

All the New Testament writers reminded us that trials will come. Peter put it like this: "In this you greatly rejoice, though now for a little while you may have had to suffer grief in all kinds of trials. These have come so that your faith — of greater

worth than gold, which perishes even though refined by fire —
may be proved genuine and may result in praise, glory and honor
when Jesus Christ is revealed" (1 Peter 1:6–7).

Paul certainly experienced trials. He knew that stress was
predictable. Hear him say, "I served the Lord with great humility
and with tears, although I was severely tested by the plots of the
Jews" (Acts 20:19). Even our Lord was not immune to the
stressful trials of life. Hear Him in the upper room saying to the
disciples, "You are those who have stood by me in my trials"
(Luke 22:28).

As Christians we face two basic types of trials: trials of
correction and trials of perfection. When we are out of the will of
God, He often allows trials to come our way in order to correct
our paths. Ask Jonah, the runaway prophet. Trials of perfection,
on the other hand, come to us when we are in the will of God,
being what God told us to be and doing what God told us to do.
Ask the disciples who climbed into the boat at Jesus' command
and found themselves in the midst of a tremendous storm. A
true test of our Christian character is how we respond when we
lose our blessings.

Yes, we will be tested as believers. Paul said that these trials
were "common to man" (1 Corinthians 10:13). But it is not nearly
as essential for us to explain life's trials theologically and
philosophically as it is for us to meet them head-on and deal
with them. Once we realize that stress is predictable, we can
move on and learn how to deal with it.

II. Stress Is Problematic
James 1:2

Just because trials — and the stress they produce — are
predictable does not mean that we should treat them lightly or
avoid facing them. Stress can be problematic. It has ruined many
relationships and many lives. Stress not only happens; it hurts.
Perhaps some of my readers could be writing this chapter, telling
how stress has cost them their health, their happiness, their
homes or perhaps their hopes.

James wrote to those who knew a great deal about stress.
They were, as we have seen, the scattered ones who had lost
their homes, their jobs and their belongings. Yet James told
them to consider it pure joy when they faced trials of "many
kinds." The Greek word translated "many kinds" in James 1:2,
ποικίλος, means "many colored" or "varied." James knew that
trials are not all alike. Some trials are job-related, some are
financial, some are domestic and some are the result of the fear
of failure. Other trials are a result of old age, guilt, competition
at school, problems at the office or day-by-day experiences in the
home. The point is, we are faced with trials of all sorts and stripes.

Some trials are natural. They come from sickness, accident,
disappointment or other painful circumstances. These trials are
natural because we live in fleshly bodies and in a sinful world.
Other trials are supernatural. They come upon us because we are
Christians. Peter reminded us that we should "not be surprised
at the painful trial you are suffering, as though something
strange were happening to you" (1 Peter 4:12). When we line up
with Christ, we line up against the present world's system.

Although stress can be problematic and destructive, there is
hope. We should find comfort in the fact that the stress of trials
is transitory. Peter said, "In this you greatly rejoice, though now

for *a little while* you may have had to suffer grief and all kinds of trials" (1 Peter 1:6, *italics added*). One of the most common phrases in the Bible is "And it came to pass." Are you faced with the stress of trials right now? This too shall pass! It is transitory. Perhaps Longfellow said it best: "The lowest ebb is the turn of the tide." In my office hangs a beautiful painting of a sunset with these inscribed words: "There has never been a sunset yet, not followed by a sunrise."

Stress is predictable, problematic — and paradoxical. It can be used to our advantage.

III. Stress Is Paradoxical
James 1:2–4

James said we should consider it pure "joy" when we face trials of many kinds. Consider it what? Joy! What kind of joy? Pure joy! Could this be a misprint? Most of us consider various kinds of trials to be a taste of Hell, not pure joy. We generally count it all joy when we avoid trials and tribulations. We hear about someone else's trial and breathe a prayer of joyful thanks that we are not faced with that problem.

Talk about a paradox! James' admonition seems diametrically opposed to the way we would naturally look at difficulties. His advice certainly seems strange. Most of us would say, "Consider it joy when you escape trials." For example, when we lived in South Florida, we said we lived in "hurricane alley." Every year during hurricane season we would do our best to dodge the massive, mighty storms that would make their way westward across the ocean toward us. We considered it joy when we escaped those trials.

The Greek word translated "consider", ἡγέομαι, is interesting. In James 1:2 it is in the aorist tense, which signifies that this joy that we read about comes after the trial. James was not saying the trial is joy. He was not advocating some sort of sadomasochism. This particular Greek word means "to think ahead, forward." Job was thinking ahead when he said, "But he knows the way that I take; when he has tested me, I will come forth as gold" (Job 23:10). Job did not consider losing his health a joy. But he looked forward to the joy that would follow his trial.

Joseph also considered — thought ahead. When revealing his identity to his brothers after many years of hurt he said, "You intended to harm me, but God intended it for good to accomplish what is now being done, the saving of many lives" (Genesis 50:20). Did Joseph consider it a joy to be in prison? No. But he knew God's hand was in his circumstances and he thought ahead.

Jesus looked beyond His suffering. Hebrews 12:2 says, "Let us fix our eyes on Jesus, the author and perfecter of our faith, who *for the joy set before him* endured the cross, scorning its shame, and sat down at the right hand of the throne of God" *(italics added)*. Did Jesus count Calvary a joy? Certainly not! But thinking ahead, He thought past Calvary and, therefore, He bore up under the stress of the cross. Do you see the point?

Have you considered it joy to be in the midst of a stressful situation? James wasn't saying that we have joy in the midst of our trials, but that we have joy in what lies ahead. It seems paradoxical, but James was saying, "There is joy in the outcome."

While writing this chapter, I flew at 30,000 feet en route to a speaking engagement. I saw James 1:2 come alive on that airplane. I was seated next to a woman who by all appearances was sophisticated, beautiful and charming. She seemed to have everything the world has to offer. But as we conversed she explained that though her husband had inherited the family fortune in business, he was hooked on cocaine. He had just spent six weeks in a treatment center in Virginia, and she was about to see him for the first time in a month and a half. She had talked with him the previous day by telephone, and he had said that the counselors at the treatment center had told him that he needed to believe in some higher power. It was my great joy to share with her who that "higher power" is and how she could know Him personally and receive the free pardoning of sin. Before we landed — with tears streaming down her face, yet with a countenance of joy — she invited Jesus Christ to be her personal Savior and Lord. Yes, she could consider it pure joy as she faced her trial and stress.

The apostle Paul wrote: "For our light and momentary troubles are achieving for us an eternal glory that far outweighs them all. So we fix our eyes not on what is seen, but on what is unseen. For what is seen is temporary, but what is unseen is eternal" (2 Corinthians 4:17–18).

It is also important to note that James said, "Consider it pure joy, ἀδελφόι" (James 1:2). The Greek word for "brothers" (ἀδελφόι) indicates that James wrote to those who shared a mutual life. His readers were brothers in the faith. It is folly to tell a lost man to consider it pure joy when he faces trials of many kinds. He will look at you as though you are crazy. This perspective on trials is only for those in the family of God, and it is closely related to the family secret we find in Romans 8:28: "And *we know* that in all things God works for the good of those who love him, who have been called according to his purpose" *(italics added)*.

Every trial can become a God-given opportunity for growing into the likeness of Jesus Christ. Oswald Chambers, the great devotional writer of the past generation, once said, "Every humiliation, everything that tries and vexes us, is God's way of cutting a deeper channel in us through which the life of Christ can flow." Yes, the stress of trials is paradoxical. James said that we should consider it joy because it is used to bring us to spiritual maturity (James 1:3-4). Stress does not have to be our foe; it can be our friend.

IV. Stress Is Purposeful
James 1:3–8

It Produces Purity

One purpose of stress is to lead us to purity. James reminded us that "the testing of your faith develops perseverance." In the Greek New Testament the word "testing" (δοκίμιον) is found only in two places: James 1:3 and 1 Peter 1:7, where it is translated "proved." "These have come," Peter wrote "so that your faith — of greater worth than gold, which perishes even though refined by fire — may be proved genuine and may result in praise, glory and honor when Jesus Christ is revealed."

Δοκίμιον can also be translated "purging." The word conveys a picture of a precious metal being heated until it is liquid and its impurities rise to the top and are scraped off. Only pure metal is left. The word also conveys a picture of a lady who goes to a fabric store, picks up a piece of fabric, and pulls it this way and that way to see if it will take the proper strain.

By using δοκίμιον, James emphasized that stress tests our faith. Our trials are for a purpose. Often they are a refining fire, testing us to see if we can hold up under pressure and conforming us to the image of Christ.

My high school chemistry teacher, Mr. Dunkelberg, was always giving us pop quizzes. Why? To prove our ability. To help us learn and grow. It is the same in the school of faith. God's purpose is for us to reach graduation day, so He allows tests along the way. And so often, just like many of my teacher's pop tests, they are unexpected.

It Produces Perseverance

Another purpose of stress is to lead us to perseverance. James said that the testing of our faith develops perseverance. The Greek word for "perseverance" (ὑπομονή) is derived from a preposition that means "under" and a verb that means "to stand fast." Thus James was saying the testing of our faith develops the staying power that will help us to stand up under other tests. The King James translators chose the word "patience," but that is a weak translation, for ὑπομονή is a much stronger word more appropriately translated "endurance," "steadfastness" or "perseverance." The word is also found in 2 Corinthians 1:6: "If we are distressed, it is for your comfort and salvation; if we are comforted, it is for your comfort, which produces in you *patient endurance* of the same sufferings we suffer" *(italics added)*. The word evokes a picture of someone under pressure who stands his ground instead of escaping.

Only a trial can prove the depth of our faith and character. Note what is being tested. What is on trial here? Us? No. Our faith! James was talking about the testing of our faith. Many people misunderstand the book of James, falsely thinking that it is an epistle of works. But before James ever mentioned works, he talked about faith. It is our faith that is put to the test. The Bible says, "Without faith it is impossible to please God" (Hebrews 11:6).

Perhaps you are undergoing this process of testing (δοκίμιον). The heat is on. Remember, the stress of trials is purposeful. It can produce purity and perseverance in your life. God is perfecting you, and you will come out stronger and sturdier than ever.

It Produces Perfection

Another purpose of stress is to lead us to perfection. "Perseverance must finish its work so that you may be mature and complete, not lacking anything" (James 1:4). Why must perseverance finish its work? So that we may be "mature" (τέλειος). This word means "to end, to carry work to its end, to become full grown."

A student goes to school to earn a diploma. Along the way, he may fail a few tests, miss a few math problems and confuse a few historical facts and dates. But all of that is incidental to finishing the course and walking across the stage to receive his diploma on graduation day. In the school of trials, we fail a few tests along the way and perhaps confuse a few facts. But all along the way, God is making us ready, maturing and completing us for that day when we will walk across the heavenly stage to receive our spiritual diplomas.

Our goal in Christian living is spiritual maturity. Yet learning to mature brings dangers and risks. There are a lot of tests along the way. I remember when our oldest daughter turned 16 and it was time to teach her to drive. (Some of our greatest private times together took place on Saturday afternoons in a big, empty parking lot where she learned to drive.) The time finally came when she obtained her driver's license and headed out on her own. The only way she could mature in her driving was for us to release her, and that involved risk. The same is true of spiritual maturity. The one who never undergoes trials will never mature in the faith. Stress is purposeful.

It Produces Prayer

Another benefit of stressful trials is that they lead us to prayer. James 1:5 puts it this way: "If any of you lacks wisdom, he should ask God." The Greek word for "wisdom" used here (σοφία) means "the practical use of knowledge." John Blanchard defined it as "the ability to discern God's hand in human circumstances and apply heavenly judgment to earthly situations."[1]

This was the burden of Paul's prayer for the church at Ephesus. "I keep asking," he wrote, "that the God of our Lord Jesus Christ, the glorious Father, may give you the Spirit of wisdom" (Ephesians 1:17). It was also his prayer for the Colossians: "We have not stopped praying for you and asking God to fill you with the knowledge of his will through all spiritual wisdom and understanding" (Colossians 1:9).

This kind of wisdom is not simply knowledge. We can read every book ever written on stress and still not know how to cope. We need to pray not to be smart, but to be wise. People going through stressful trials need godly wisdom more than anything else. When we go through trials, we have a tendency to lose perspective and direction. It becomes so easy to take our focus off the Lord and put our focus on circumstances; we forget that the wisdom we need originates with God.

The greatest need of modern man is wisdom (σοφία). Think about this with me. In many ways our generation is the most prolific of all generations. We have more college graduates. In our day and age, it is not enough simply to have a bachelor's degree. It is increasingly important to have master's degrees to excel in our chosen professions. Knowledge is exploding. We travel farther and fly higher and faster than any previous generation in history. We accumulate data as never before. The computer age is advancing in such a way that information becomes outdated with virtually every passing minute. But while such knowledge is increasing, wisdom is often lacking. Many lives are in shambles. Suicide rates are higher than ever before. Morals are at a record low. Divorce claims more than half of those who are married. In many ways the world is on the brink of chaos. And to such a generation James 1:5 says, "If any of you lacks wisdom, he should ask God, who gives generously to all without finding fault, and it will be given to him."

To whom does God give this wisdom? James said He gives it to those who ask. We do not get σοφία in school or from practical experience. It is God's gift to us. God is a giving God and He is not stingy with wisdom. He gives it generously, in the words of James, but we must ask for it. James used a present active imperative form of Greek for "ask," which means we are to "keep on asking." Our requests are not to be just shots in the dark, from the hip or off the cuff. When we face trials and need wisdom, we are to continue to ask God for it with a repetitive urgency.

James was not saying that if we lack wisdom we should sit down and think about it. No. He didn't say we need to learn more theology or keep our noses in textbooks. He said we should ask. This is why so many Christians lack wisdom. They are too proud simply to ask. If God would tell us to do something hard, we'd each be first in line to volunteer, but when He tells us to humble ourselves and ask Him for this gift, many of us balk.

When King Solomon was about to take control of the throne, God made an incredible proposition to him: "Ask for whatever you want me to give you" (1 Kings 3:5). Do you remember what Solomon answered? "So give your servant a discerning heart to govern your people and to distinguish between right and wrong. For who is able to govern this great people of yours?" (1 Kings 3:9). Solomon asked for wisdom! He could have had anything he wanted, but he asked for wisdom. He chose the best, and God threw in the rest.

Here is a scenario. You have a crisis. It creates stress. So what do you do? Call the doctor and order pills? Make another appointment with the counselor? Go out and buy the best self-help book? Or do you pray? Often we do the best thing last. Of course, there's nothing wrong with going to a doctor, seeking counsel or reading. But first we should call upon God and pray. It is no coincidence that the middle verse of the Bible, Psalm 118:8, reads, "It is better to take refuge in the Lord than to trust in man."

James 4:2 says, "You do not have, because you do not ask God." Since the devil cannot keep God from answering our prayers, what does he do? He seeks to keep us from asking. He lies to us, saying, "You are not worthy to ask God." He tells us to help ourselves first and then go to God as a last resort.

Consider people under pressure at the office because of an unfair boss. If all they have to rely on is human wisdom, they will complicate the matter with confusion. They need God's wisdom to see that their situation may be orchestrated, or at least allowed by God, to make them more Christlike. The point of their friction may be allowed by God because He is working on specific parts of their lives that He wants to perfect.

God gives us σοφία wisdom without finding fault. Some people give gifts with all sorts of strings attached, and sometimes use the giving of those gifts as opportunities to belittle, insult or rebuke the recipients (as if the givers had bought the right to do so). But not God. He will never say, "You made your bed; now lie in it." He will never say, "I told you so." When we ask God for wisdom, He will never look at us with crossed arms, clenched fists or pointed fingers. He will give wisdom without finding fault.

How we ask is important too. James 1:6 says, "But when he asks, he must believe and not doubt, because he who doubts is like a wave of the sea, blown and tossed by the wind." There is a condition attached to God's granting us wisdom. He gives it to those who ask in faith. We must believe and not doubt. The Greek word for "doubt" (διακρίνω) is a compound of two words that mean "through" and "to separate." Διακρίνω conveys a sense of being divided against oneself. One incident in the life of Peter is a picture of διακρίνω. He walked on the water and then sank. Jesus said to him, "Why did you doubt?" (Matthew 14:31). He was asking, "Why did you think twice?"

We are to ask in faith. Often we hear someone say, "I asked God, but nothing happened." Perhaps he overlooked the condition: "When he asks, he must believe." No wonder Paul wrote, "We live by faith, not by sight" (2 Corinthians 5:7). Jesus put it like this: "Therefore I tell you, whatever you ask for in prayer, believe that you have received it, and it will be yours" (Mark 11:24). Jesus did not mean that God will give us everything for which we ask. The idea of "demanding of God" or "claiming" things from God is not at issue here. The issue is faith.

Where is faith found? "Faith comes from hearing the message, and the message is heard through the word of Christ" (Romans 10:17). Faith is born of the Word of God when it is quickened to our hearts by the Holy Spirit.

James likened the man who asks without faith to one who is blown by the wind and tossed by the waves. Perhaps you have been in the midst of the ocean and experienced its constant rolling. I enjoy fishing in the Atlantic Ocean off the coast of Fort Lauderdale. When the waves are rolling, it is difficult to keep the boat on course. Likewise, doubt leaves one unsettled. If we want smoother sailing through life, we must believe that God knows what is best for us, and by faith ask Him for wisdom.

The doubting man has no sense of direction in life. James 1:7-8 says, "That man should not think he will receive anything from the Lord; he is a double-minded man, unstable in all he does." The one who doubts will not receive wisdom from the Lord. Rather, he will simply be the victim of greater stress. Ineffective prayer is due in part to what James referred to as "double-mindedness" (δίψυχος). This Greek word means "two souls" — two thought patterns, with a soul divided between faith and the world. The doubting man has a divided heart. He is trying to serve two masters. It is as though a part of him shouts, "I believe," and the other part cries out, "I doubt." James said that this type of individual is unstable in all he does. In other words, doubt affects every area of his life. Unstable in his relationship with God, he cannot live by faith and is therefore unstable at home, in the workplace, in social situations and everywhere else. How important it is to have God's wisdom to cope with life's stresses.

The stress of trials is predictable, problematic, paradoxical and purposeful. Our greatest need is wisdom. Where do we get it? We need to ask. Who gives it? God. How? In response to our faith. How will He give? Generously.

The psalmist put it like this: "The fear of the Lord is the beginning of wisdom" (Psalm 111:10). The man or woman who has no reverence for God is lacking true wisdom. He or she may have an IQ higher than 150, but no wisdom. Wisdom does not come from Plato, Aristotle, Socrates, Kierkegaard or any other philosopher of renown. Look again at the source of wisdom: "If any of you lacks wisdom, he should ask God, who gives generously to all without finding fault, and it will be given to him" (James 1:5). Knowledge is the accumulation of facts. Wisdom is the ability to deal with the facts and use them in practical ways. Almost anyone can gain knowledge, but only those who seek God can gain true wisdom.

V. Stress Is Profitable
James 1:9–12

George Sweeting wrote, "A Christian is like a tea bag. He is not worth much until he has been through some hot water."[2] Yes, trials are profitable. James 1:9–12 describes three men: the man with poverty, the man with plenty and the man with pressure. The trials God allows have a way of bringing us all to one level. When I was a pastor, I visited many homes to meet the needs of families going through trials. I have driven up to million-dollar waterfront homes behind big iron gates, and I have driven up to little frame homes in neighborhoods where safety requires iron bars on the windows. I have been with those in poverty, I have been with those in plenty and I have been with those under pressure. I have seen how stress and trials have become profitable for those who have learned to deal with them. Let's briefly examine each type of person.

The Person with Poverty

James 1:9 says, "The brother in humble circumstances ought to take pride in his high position." The word translated "humble" is the Greek word ταπεινός. It means "lowly" and describes one who is low on the socioeconomic scale, one who is relatively poor and powerless. The world may think that such a person is not worth much, but God says he is worth very much. Here is a mystery of the Christian life: The last shall be first and the low shall be high.

When I read James 1:9, I think of Noah. No one encouraged him. No one cheered for him. He was lampooned, mocked, laughed at, scorned and neglected. But God exalted him.

James wrote that the brother in humble circumstances

should take pride in his "high position." What position? As followers of Christ we belong to a heavenly realm. We are of great worth to God, and we should rejoice in the spiritual things we can never lose. The missionary martyr Jim Elliot said it best: "He is no fool who gives what he cannot keep to gain what he cannot lose."

An impoverished person must look beyond physical circumstances and abide in spiritual values. Paul did, and he wrote, "But our citizenship is in heaven. And we eagerly await a Savior from there, the Lord Jesus Christ" (Philippians 3:20).

The Person with Plenty

The early church had both people in poverty and people who had plenty. The fellowship included not only those in great physical and financial need, but also some of the wealthiest people in Jerusalem. There were men like Joseph of Arimathaea, Nicodemus and Barnabas, the property owner.

James 1:10–11 says, "The one who is rich should take pride in his low position, because he will pass away like a wild flower. For the sun rises with scorching heat and withers the plant; its blossom falls and its beauty is destroyed. In the same way, the rich man will fade away even while he goes about his business." James was saying that while those who are rich according to the world's standards may take pride in their possessions, the Christian person of plenty takes pride in his spiritual position. He knows that the grass withers and the flower fades, that treasures laid up on earth will rust and be devoured by moths.

For believers, poverty is temporary and so is prosperity, especially in comparison to the eternal glory that is ours in Christ Jesus. Therefore, neither poverty nor plenty makes for happiness in the Christian life. Jesus reminds us that "a man's life does not consist in the abundance of his possessions"

(Luke 12:15). Those with plenty should rejoice in the spiritual things they cannot lose. If your happiness is based on your position in Christ, you can never lose that. If your happiness is found in your possessions, then you should heed James 1:11.

The man in poverty, who in the eyes of the world is not worth much, should find joy in his relationship with the Lord who elevates him to a high position. The man in plenty should remember that his only lasting security is not in stocks or bonds or properties, but in his relationship with the Lord. In dealing with stress, both men should look at their lives from a heavenly perspective, not an earthly perspective. The gospel has a leveling effect. In Jericho, Jesus and His disciples met two men on the same day. One was impoverished and the other had plenty. To Bartimaeus, the poverty-stricken blind beggar on the roadside, the disciples said, "Rise" (Mark 10:49 KJV). To Zacchaeus, the wealthy tax collector who had climbed the tree, Jesus said, "Come down" (Luke 19:5). Do you see the parallel to James 1:9–10?

The Person with Pressure

For the rich and poor alike, stress is profitable for the person under pressure. James 1:12 says, "Blessed is the man who perseveres under trial, because when he has stood the test, he will receive the crown of life that God has promised to those who love him." Satan wants to use trials to cause us to stumble, but God allows them in order for us to stand. The word perseveres is the verb form of the noun we saw in James 1:3. It means "staying power." Perseverance is not the morbid response of a person who sits down, bows his head and passively endures rebukes and testings. Perseverance is the response of the person who bears up under stressful circumstances. Perhaps you find yourself buried under trials at this time. What should you do? Some say you should run away. But James' advice was, "Stand up under them." So hold your ground.

Happy is the person who perseveres under trial, who stands his ground. Why is he happy? Because after the test, he will receive the crown of life. In the ancient Grecian games, a wreath was placed on the victor's head as a sign of honor and victory. This "crown" (στέφανος) is what Paul had in mind when he wrote in one of his last letters to Timothy from a prison cell in Rome: "I have fought the good fight, I have finished the race, I have kept the faith. Now there is in store for me *the crown of righteousness*, which the Lord, the righteous Judge, will award to me on that day — and not only to me, but also to all who have longed for his appearing" (2 Timothy 4:7–8, *italics added*). The man or woman who stands firm will receive this crown of life. God has a special reward for patient sufferers. In the end, stress is certainly profitable.

As a pastor, I have watched many men and women face difficulties and even death. Some time ago I went through the traumatic experience of watching my best friend, Gene Whiddon, die a long and agonizing death. I watched him die as he had lived, persevering under trial. Never once did I hear him complain. During our last visit, I read with him the promises of God concerning the great Marriage Supper of the Lamb and the Crown of Life which the Lord, the righteous Judge, will give us on "that day." As I left the hospital room and looked back for a parting smile, his final words to me were, "I'll save you a place at the table."

Echoing the theme of James 1:12, the Apostle John wrote these inspired words from God: "Do not be afraid of what you are about to suffer. I tell you, the devil will put some of you in prison to test you, and you will suffer persecution...Be faithful, even to the point of death, and I will give you the crown of life" (Revelation 2:10).

No wonder Fanny Crosby, who endured the stress of blindness for a lifetime, said:

Great things He has taught us, great things He has done,
And great our rejoicing through Jesus the Son;
But purer, and higher, and greater will be
Our wonder, our transport, when Jesus we see.

Stress...the menace of modern man. How do we handle it? Remember, it is predictable. It is a question of when, not if. It is not going to go away. None of us is immune. Stress is also problematic. If we do not deal with it, stress is destructive. Stress is also paradoxical. We can count it as joy because we know that the final, eternal outcome will be glorious. Stress is also purposeful. God is testing us, putting us through the furnace so that we might come out as pure gold. Finally, stress is profitable. Think ahead to the crown of life!

The word victory implies a struggle. Consider the struggle of a butterfly to emerge from its cocoon. Once there was a little boy who found a cocoon attached to a small branch of a tree. He took the branch home and kept it securely in his room. When spring came, the butterfly began to struggle to escape from its prison. Wanting to help, the boy found a pair of small scissors and made a slight incision in the cocoon. Soon the butterfly emerged in all of its radiant beauty. But it never flew! Having escaped all the struggle to emerge from the cocoon, the muscles of its wings never developed. The boy's good intentions robbed the butterfly of its power to soar. Yes, "Perseverance must finish its work so that you may be mature and complete, not lacking anything" (James 1:4).

....
⊛ **CHAPTER TWO** ⊛
....

RELATIVISM: THE RELIGION OF MODERN MAN
JAMES 1:13-17

I. The Cause of Temptation (James 1:13–14)
II. The Course of Temptation (James 1:15)
III. The Caution of Temptation (James 1:16–17)

James' letter to the scattered believers of the first-century world is as up-to-date with the pressures facing modern man as any best-selling book currently on the market. In fact, we face all 13 of the major issues with which the epistle deals. For example, James 1:13–17 addresses relativism, the new religion that seems to be sweeping the western world, as we have entered the third millennium.

Professor Allan Bloom, author of the best-selling book *The Closing of the American Mind,* spoke of asking his undergraduate class at the University of Chicago to identify an evil person. Bloom said that not one student could do so. Evil did not exist as a category in their minds. The professor said, "Our inability to recognize and identify evil is a sign of grave danger in our society."

Ted Turner, who pioneered the explosion of cable television, said in a meeting of the National Newspaper Association, "The Ten Commandments are out of date and irrelevant to current global problems. Nobody here pays much attention to them because they are too old." He also told the Dallas Morning News that "Christianity is for losers!"

Morality is almost a forgotten word in our generation. Few people speak of temptation. This is the day of relativism, which simply means that many people believe there are no moral absolutes. Consequently, they have no restraints. Even more and more of God's people are succumbing to temptations and refusing to live according to God's absolutes.

Relativism is escalating at a rapid pace and major moral scandals are surfacing in every field of endeavor. Well-known sports figures and role models have been exposed for gambling on their own teams or for having illicit sex with countless partners. Presidential hopefuls have drowned in the murky waters of immorality. High-level business professionals who thought they were above the law have landed in prison. And some high-level spokesmen for the Christian faith have been exposed for their double standards. In such a moral climate, James' words about temptation are appropriate. His caution echoes through the corridors of time into the twenty-first century: "Don't be deceived, my dear brothers" (James 1:16).

Having dealt with external trials, James turns now to internal temptations. The root word translated "trials" (noun form) in James 1:2 is translated "tempted" (verb form) in James 1:13. The context of these words provides the key to understanding the difference. The context of James 1:2 is a discussion of the testing of our faith. The context of James 1:13 is a discussion of our propensity to sin.

In his discussion of relativism, James addressed three important points: the cause of temptation, the course of temptation and the caution of temptation.

I. The Cause of Temptation
James 1:13–14

What is the cause — the source, the origin — of temptation that comes our way? Most of us would quickly say it comes from without, that it originates with God, Satan or certain circumstances. But listen carefully to what James says: "When tempted, no one should say, 'God is tempting me.' For God cannot be tempted by evil, nor does he tempt anyone" (James 1:13).

The Greek word James used to reveal that God "cannot be tempted" is ἀπείραστος. (It is not used anywhere else in the New Testament.) This Greek word includes a prefix that means "not" or "un." God is untemptable. Since He is not experienced in evil (Jesus never sinned), He cannot tempt us toward it. Satan figured wrong when he tempted Jesus in the wilderness. Not one of his enticements appealed to the Lord Jesus. He knew no sin (see 2 Corinthians 5:21; Hebrews 4:15; 1 John 3:5).

Many people blame God for their own sin. They say, "God created everything; therefore it stands to reason that He created this impulse within me to do evil. Therefore, He created sin. He is ultimately responsible." This line of reasoning would conclude, "I can't help it; God just made me this way." This argument is often used by the adulterer or the homosexual.

From the garden of Eden to the present day, men and women have always tried to evade personal responsibility. Adam said, "Not guilty! The woman is to blame." Eve said, "Not guilty! The devil made me do it." And most of us are no different when it comes to facing the cause of our temptations.

Satan, however, is not the cause of our temptations. James said, "Each one is tempted when, *by his own evil desire*, he is dragged away" (James 1:14, *italics added*). In this entire discussion of temptation, Satan is never mentioned. In the garden of Eden, all he did was toss the desire to Eve to doubt God's word and she took it from there; he's never seen again in the garden.

Still others blame sin on circumstances. They say, "It's not necessarily God's fault, or the devil's fault, or our fault. It's just one of those things. We were just in a situation where we shouldn't have been." Some blame sin on their environment. Perhaps they live in a city where drugs and immorality run rampant. But it is not the place...not the situation...not our peers...that cause temptations.

James wanted us to see that we should never blame God, the devil or circumstances. What then is the cause? Temptation comes from two places: an internal source and an external force. James 1:14 says, "Each one is tempted when, by his own evil desire, he is dragged away and enticed." When our internal desire to do wrong connects with outward enticement, sin is born in our lives.

An Internal Source

The Greek word, ἐπιθυμία, means a "strong desire directed toward an object." In James 1:14 ἐπιθυμία is translated "evil desire" in the NIV. It is often translated "lust" in the English New Testament, but its meaning is not necessarily limited to physical, sexual lust. In fact, Jesus used ἐπιθυμία when He said, "I have *eagerly desired* to eat this Passover with you before I suffer" (Luke 22:15, *italics added*). And the word is translated "intense longing" in 1 Thessalonians 2:17.

Many desires are good. The desire to eat and drink is good when kept within God's guidelines. The desire for rest is good within limits. Within God's boundaries the desire for sex is good. The problem comes when we want to satisfy our desires outside the parameter of God's will. For example, eating is commendable, but gluttony is a sin. Sleep is essential, but laziness is a sin. Sexual activity within the marriage relationship is good, but adultery is a sin. Many desires are not evil in and of themselves.

But when desire — an internal source — attaches itself to an evil object, it draws us out and away from our place of security. In the words of James, we are "dragged away" (ἐξέλκω). This Greek word is a compound that comes from a preposition meaning "out of" and a word meaning "to be drawn by an inward power."[1] When we meditate on James 1:14, we can picture ourselves living in a secure place. We begin to allow a desire to lead us contrary to the Word of God. The desire draws us out from our place of shelter and security and leaves us vulnerable to sin.

Note that the Bible says "each one" is dragged away. Temptation is personal. It is an individual matter within each of us. We are all familiar with this internal source — this desire within us. And each one is responsible. We cannot blame God, Satan or circumstances. When there is no evil desire, there is no temptation. The internal source draws us away and causes us to want to play outside God's boundaries.

An External Force

If the internal source is desire, then the external force is deception. When the internal source and the external force connect, the result is sin.

James said that once desire becomes evil, it causes us to be "enticed" (James 1:14). The Greek word for "enticed" (δελεάζω) is a present middle participle that means "being baited or deceived."[2] "Hooked on" finds its origin in δελεάζω. Have you ever heard the expression, "He is hooked on drugs"? Or, "He or she is hooked on sex"? Δελεάζω appears only three times in the New Testament. In 2 Peter 2:14 it is translated "seduced."

A number of years ago, I caught a seven-pound black bass in Kentucky Lake. That fish illustrates δελεάζω. I took a beautiful plastic worm, stuck a hook into it and bent the hook so it could not be seen. I attached it to transparent fishing line, dropped it by some bushes near the lake's edge and jiggled it along the bottom. The big bass, which was lying in a hole, suddenly saw this delicious-looking worm in front of him. Now think about it. He had a desire (an internal source). Therefore, when the external force came along, it was more than he could handle. The worm looked so delicious...and he swallowed it! Then he was dragged away out of his hole of security. I set the hook and took him out of his environment into the boat and to eventual death. I fooled that bass. I enticed him with a baited hook.

All of us have been hooked by the world's allurements in just the same way. They looked so good, so attractive, so satisfying, so fulfilling, but it was all deception. You took the bait and got hooked. My fish would never have swum out of his hole to bite a bare hook. I had to hide the hook, disguise it and make it look attractive. Temptation has a way of appealing to our natural desires and attracting us while hiding the fact that it is a trap that will eventually harm or even destroy us.

No one put the worm in the fish's mouth. He came out of the hole because of his own desire, and he took the bait. Sin never starts with the bait; it always starts with a desire. I have dropped a worm in front of many black bass that did not bite. The one mounted on my wall had a desire. In the garden of Eden, sin began with that selfish desire in Eve's heart. Then came the external force. Satan made his move, and she "saw that the fruit of the tree was good for food and pleasing to the eye, and also desirable for gaining wisdom" (Genesis 3:6). The rest is history.

The same series of events happened to King David. His sin with Bathsheba came about because of his internal desire to play outside God's boundaries. David was out of God's will. He was in the palace when, as the Bible says, it was "the time when kings go off to war" (2 Samuel 11:1). So what happened? Satan baited the hook with an external force. Her name was Bathsheba. And King David took the bait.

Do you think for one minute that King David, the man who had a heart after God's own heart, would have done what he did had he looked ahead and seen the results? No! Neither would some of us who "took the bait." If you are being tempted to sin at this very moment, James screams at you, "Don't be deceived!" (James 1:16). There is a deadly hook in that worm. The bait is keeping some of us from seeing the consequences of sin.

When we grab the bait, the hidden hook grabs us. The hook itself is not sin; it is sin's penalty.[3] Sin takes place when desire and deception connect. We are lured out of our position by desire, just as the fish was lured out of his hole. Then we take the bait when it comes by and we get hooked. How important it is for us, with God's help, to master our desires. Temptation is so subtle.

I have seen desire and deception connect when married men begin to leave the Word of God closed. Their desires get out of line with God's desires. They start reading materials they shouldn't read, and very subtly their evil desires drag them out of their place of security. Perhaps a secretary walks by in the office. She may have been there for years, but now he sees her as bait. He begins to flirt with her. He takes the bait and is hooked.

If it were not for evil desire, Satan would never gain a victory over us by dangling hooks in front of us. How vital it is that we stay in the Word and remain constant in prayer so that our desires continue to be God's desires.

Sin begins in the heart. Jesus says, "What comes out of a man is what makes him 'unclean.' For from within, out of men's hearts, come evil thoughts, sexual immorality, theft, murder, adultery, greed, malice, deceit, lewdness, envy, slander, arrogance and folly. All these evils come from inside and make a man 'unclean'" (Mark 7:20–23). What a man needs is a new nature, a change of desires from within. Churches can try to get legislation passed that will close every adult bookstore and nude bar in their cities. But the problem within man will remain.

It is not a sin, however, to see the baited hook. It is not a sin to be tempted. The sin is born when the internal source (desire) and the external force (deception) come together, and we take the bait. For example, let's say that two men are walking down the street. They pass an enticement — a hooker. (Why do you think they are called "hookers?") The prostitute smiles and gives them that "come-on" look. Both men see the bait. Why does one take it and the other walk on by on the other side? It is because of the men's internal desires. One has desires that are within the boundaries of God because he has fed his spirit with the Word. The other has desires that are outside the boundaries of God because he has fed his spirit with pornographic magazines. Sin is conceived in the heart. Jesus said, "It is what comes out of a man that makes him 'unclean'" (Mark 7:15).

The evening before the crucifixion, in the garden of Gethsemane, the Lord Jesus gave the inner three — Peter, James, John — some good advice. "*Watch and pray*," He said, "so that you will not fall into temptation" (Matthew 26:41, *italics added*). Prayer has to do with the internal source, our desires. Prayer connects us with God so that our desires can become more like His desires. This is why the psalmist wrote, "Delight yourself in the Lord and he will give you the desires of your heart" (Psalm 37:4). Watching has to do with the external force, the deception. We are to be alert, to watch out. The bait has a hook in it! If we look closely enough, we can see it. We must watch and pray so that we will not fall into temptation.

The cause of temptation is not found in any externals. It is not found in God, in the devil or in circumstances. James said that each of us is tempted when, "by his own evil desires, he is dragged away and enticed" (James 1:14).

II. The Course of Temptation
James 1:15

It is imperative for us as believers not simply to examine the cause of temptation, but also to examine its course — where it leads us. James cautioned us to look down the road and see where sin ends...in defeat and death.

Temptation is like a weed that grows unchecked and destroys. A weed has three parts: a root, a shoot and a fruit. A root left untouched produces a shoot that bursts out into the open and produces fruit. The progression is obvious. It is the same with temptation. The root of temptation is a selfish desire. The shoot of temptation is a sinful decision. The fruit of temptation is a sure defeat. James 1:15 puts it this way: "Then, after desire has conceived, it gives birth to sin; and sin, when it is full-grown, gives birth to death." This law of Scripture is just as certain as the law of gravity.

Note that verse 15 begins with the word "then." Sin doesn't just happen out of the clear blue. When desire and deception connect, then the sin they create brings forth death. The course of temptation is progressive. It goes from root to shoot to fruit.

The Root...A Selfish Desire

"Desire" (ἐπιθυμία) is a strong urge, a craving of the soul. There is nothing wrong with a desire. In fact, a desire can be productive when it is satisfied within the boundaries of the Bible and its laws for happiness and well-being. But James was talking about selfish desires.

When the internal source (desire) and the external force (deception) come together, conception takes place. Conception requires the participation of two parties. The word for "conceive" (συλλαμβάνω) is derived from a conjunction that means "together" and a verb that means "to take or to bring." There, this compound Greek word means "to achieve conception." When we begin to desire that which is outside of God's boundaries and we take the bait that comes by, conception takes place and sin has its root. When the internal source and the external force are brought together, sin is conceived.

Note that even though this baby — sin — is still in the womb, it is growing. What is James telling us? Sin is present in the heart before it ever bursts into the open.

The more one seeks to satisfy a selfish inner desire, the more his craving grows. Talk to a man seeking to find purpose and meaning in life by satisfying desires that are outside God's boundaries and ask him a few questions. Ask him how much money is enough, and he will tell you, "Just a little more." Ask him how much sex is enough, and he will tell you, "Just a little more." Ask him how much dope is enough, and he will tell you, "Just a little more." Ask him how much recognition and applause is enough, and he will tell you, "Just a little more." A man without Christ is never satisfied. Only God can satisfy him permanently, but he keeps on disregarding God's boundaries. A man without God keeps on trying to find satisfaction elsewhere, and all the while the root of selfish desire is breaking out of the ground and forming a shoot.

When a selfish desire enters the mind and takes root, the root should be removed immediately, or it will soon produce fruit. The moment evil thoughts come, we should surrender our minds to Christ. We may need to do that many times a day. We each should pray, "Lord, my mind is Yours. Take over and put Your thoughts into me." If possible, we should open our Bibles immediately and feed on God's thoughts. Paul said, "Let this mind be in you, which was also in Christ Jesus" (Philippians 2:5 KJV).

The Shoot...A Sinful Decision

The root of selfish desire will soon give way to the shoot. Sin begins when the internal source and the external force connect. Sin is the union of a selfish desire and an act of the will.

The Bible says that desire will eventually "give birth" to sin. The Greek word τίκτω, translated "give birth" in James 1:15, means "to bring forth as fruit from a seed."[4] The word suggests a picture of a child dwelling for awhile in the mother's womb and finally making its appearance into the world.[5] The evil desire cannot stay hidden within forever, any more than a child can stay in a mother's womb indefinitely. If the root is left untouched, sooner or later a shoot appears. That is why the Bible says, "Be sure that your sin will find you out" (Numbers 32:23).

Some people believe that because they haven't committed the act of sin, their continuing to think about it is perfectly all right. What a foolish thought. Our selfish desires give birth to sin.

That word "sin" (ἁμαρτία) means "to miss the mark." Greek writers used this word in three primary ways. In the physical dimension it could describe an archer who aims at the bull's-eye, lets go of the arrow but misses the target. He misses the mark. In the mental dimension, it could describe a student who sits down to take a test and fails. He misses the mark. In the spiritual dimension, it could describe a man who knows a certain standard of behavior, yet falls below it. He, too, misses the mark.

The best definition of sin is found in the Bible. First John 3:4 says, "Sin is lawlessness." It is the natural result of an evil desire left untouched. If a selfish desire is a root, then a sinful decision is certainly the shoot.

The Fruit...A Sure Defeat

There is a progression here. There is a stage of conception, a stage of growth and a stage of birth. But note something about this birth: Sin "gives birth to death" (James 1:15). Stillborn!

James is warning his readers to look ahead to where sin ends. "The wages of sin is death" (Romans 6:23). Ultimately, sin leads to physical death, but it also means the death of dreams, relationships, ambitions, reputations and everything else that is good. Sin never brings anything permanently good into our lives.

The Greek word for "death" ($\theta\acute{\alpha}\nu\alpha\tauo\varsigma$) means "separation." In physical death, the spirit is separated from the body. In eternal death, the spirit of man is separated from God forever. James was saying, "Sin, when it is full-grown, gives birth to separation."

Don't we already know that separation is the fruit of yielding to temptation? How many men and women have been down this road of sin and found that it ends in separation? Most of us never think about the consequences when we take the bait. But we soon find out that sin brings death and separation from all that is good for us. Some of us have known men and women who took the bait, got hooked and died. Others have experienced the death of hopes, health, home or happiness.

The chain reaction moves from the root (selfish desire) to the shoot (sinful decision) to the fruit (sure defeat). Its progression is seen throughout the Bible, beginning with Adam and Eve. Their fall began with a selfish desire to eat the forbidden fruit. It continued with a sinful decision to eat, and it ended with sure defeat — they were expelled from the garden. David's fall, too, began with a selfish desire — a lust for Bathsheba. It continued with a sinful decision, and it eventually brought sure defeat and death.

Many people in our culture today have succumbed to addictions through this subtle process of temptation. How does one become addicted to drugs? Perhaps he buys the argument of relativism, that there are no absolutes and, therefore, no restraints. Then he sees the bait at a party. Important people in the city, the movers and shakers, are doing it. It looks so attractive. It seems like the way to be accepted. So the internal source and the external force get together, and the person takes the bait. Now he has the shoot, not just the root. He comes out into the open and keeps going, only to find that the shoot brings forth the fruit. He is hooked. He is no longer in control of his passions and has lost all restraint. The same type of process occurs with any kind of addiction, whether it be sexual, monetary or another sort.

How do people deal with temptation? Often the same way they deal with weeds in their yards. Some try to deal with the fruit; that is, they just take the garden shears and cut off the tops. But within a few days the weeds are growing back. When dealing with sin, they say, "We'll just stop," but they only deal with externals and never get to the root. Others try to deal with the shoot. They mow their weeds down to the ground so their yards look good...for awhile. To deal with sin, they avoid adult bookstores and nude bars so that on the surface everything looks good, but they do not get to the root that is internal.

The effective way to deal with temptation is to deal not with the fruit or the shoot, but with the root. There is only one way to deal with the root: Let God take it out. God must change our desires and give us a new nature. The spiritually victorious life is an exchanged life, not a changed life. It doesn't just change its outward moral standards. Rather, Jesus exchanges the old sinful heart for one that is brand-new.

Why was Satan such a failure at luring Christ into temptation? Think about it. He wiggled the bait in front of our Lord. The external force was there. Christ had been fasting for

40 days, and Satan was tempting Him to turn the stone into bread. But there was no lustful desire in the heart of Christ. The Lord Jesus never considered taking Satan's bait because His desires were in line with the Father's.

How did Christ deal with the temptations? He answered all three of the temptation attempts in the same way: "It is written" (Matthew 4:4, 7, 10). Our Lord knew and used the Word of God. The only way we can tell that bait is a trap is to know and use God's Word. As D. L. Moody wrote in the flyleaf of his Bible, "This book will keep you from sin or sin will keep you from this book."

The real battlefield is in the mind. This is why Paul, describing those he called enemies of the cross, wrote, "Their destiny is destruction, their god is their stomach, and their glory is in their shame. Their mind is on earthly things" (Philippians 3:19). Then, in Colossians 3:2 he wrote, "Set your minds on things above, not on earthly things." And in Philippians 4:8 he said, "Whatever is true, whatever is noble, whatever is right, whatever is pure, whatever is lovely, whatever is admirable… think about such things." It is dangerous and potentially damaging to let your mind feed on impure thoughts. Why? Because those thoughts become the root of sin.

As believers, we can overcome temptation with God's help. When I was converted to Christ on a cold, January morning in 1965, a saintly old gentleman stuck a piece of paper in my hand and said, "Son, memorize this verse. You are going to need it." When I got home, I took the crumbled piece of paper from my pocket and found these words scribbled on it: "1 Corinthians 10:13." I quickly looked up and memorized that verse and have used it repeatedly over the years. "No temptation has seized you except what is common to man. And God is faithful; he will not let you be tempted beyond what you can bear. But when you are tempted, he will also provide a way out so that you can stand up under it."

III. The Caution of Temptation
James 1:16–17

James concluded his words about relativism and temptation with a flashing yellow caution light: "Don't be deceived" (James 1:16). The Greek word for "deceived" means "to take or go off course." The word suggests a picture of a ship that strays off course and wanders away from its designated route. It is possible for Christians to be deceived and get off course; many of us are. James was speaking to believers; it is important to note that James addressed his caution to "my dear brothers." James wanted us to make sure we are not deceived about sin, the Savior and salvation.

Don't Be Deceived About Sin

Many people today are deceived regarding the issue of sin. Sin has become a forgotten word. It is looked upon as an archaic idea in modern secular education. In an atmosphere of widespread belief that there are no absolutes and no restraints, should we be surprised that so many do what seems right in their own eyes? The cry of our society is, "If it feels good, do it." But James wrote, "Don't be deceived."

Centuries ago Augustine wrote that it was "difficult to convince people indulging in illicit sex that they were sinning."[6] Surely our current culture is echoing those same words. Sex is a beautiful thing. It is God's gift to men and women. However, used wrongly, it is destructive above all other things. Why? Because sexual sin is different from other sins. It is the sole sin one commits not only against God, but also against himself. Some would argue that sin is sin and that one sin cannot be differentiated from another. They say, "It is all the same in God's eyes." Is it?

Paul said, "Flee from sexual immorality. All other sins a man commits are outside his body, but he who sins sexually sins against his own body" (1 Corinthians 6:18). Remember, our bodies are the dwelling place of the Holy Spirit. The church edifice is not. Why is it that some would never think of committing fornication on a communion table and yet do it with their own bodies?

Don't Be Deceived About the Savior

James wrote, "Every good and perfect gift is from above, coming down from the Father of the heavenly lights, who does not change like shifting shadows" (James 1:17). God is the author of all that is good. He is not the cause of sin and suffering. Do not be deceived into thinking that anything good comes from anywhere or anyone but God.

Two different Greek words used in verse 17 have to do with the gift and the giving. One, δόσις, has to do with the act of giving. The other, δώρημα, refers to the gift itself. In other words, both the act of giving and the gift are good. The value of a gift can be greatly diminished by the way in which it is given. If the one you love simply tosses a gift in your direction as though it were an obligation, that takes away from the joy of receiving the gift. Therefore, the act of giving is as important as the gift itself. When God gives a blessing, He does it in a loving way.

James wrote that the Lord is the "Father of the heavenly lights, who does not change like shifting shadows" (James 1:17). Life may have shadows, but they are never caused by His turning. Go out tonight and stand under a street light. If you stand directly under it, there will be no shadow. Take one step away from the light and see the shadow in front of you. It is caused by your moving. Take a few more steps and what happens? The shadow grows. If you go far enough, you will be in total darkness. You will have removed yourself from the environment of the light. Shadows occur when things come between a surface and a light. Shadows are not caused by the light's movement. If there are shadows in our lives, they are not there because God (the light) has moved. They are there because we have allowed something to come between us and God. James told us not to be deceived about the Savior.

One of the joys of my private devotional life is to repeat many wonderful hymns of praise back to the Father. I suppose the hymn I have prayed the most is:

> *Great is Thy faithfulness, O God, my Father,*
> *There is no shadow of turning with Thee;*
> *Thou changest not, Thy compassions, they fail not;*
> *As Thou hast been, Thou forever wilt be.*
> *Great is Thy faithfulness! Great is Thy faithfulness!*
> *Morning by morning new mercies I see;*
> *All I have needed, Thy hand hath provided;*
> *Great is Thy faithfulness, Lord, unto me.*[7]

Don't Be Deceived About Salvation

What is the first step toward victory over temptation? It is salvation, the reception of a new, God-given nature. The devil never gives us good gifts. They may look enticing, but they have hooks in them and they result in death and separation. In effect James said, "Don't be deceived. Don't take the devil's bait. God has the good gift of salvation to give to anyone who asks. Every good and perfect gift is from above; it comes from the Father of lights."

Note that the gift of salvation comes "from above." It is supernatural. Jesus called it the "new birth." Salvation changes our desires. It causes old things to go, and new things to come

(2 Corinthians 5:17). We begin to hate things we used to love, and love things we used to hate. We receive this good gift, eternal life, through faith in Jesus Christ our Lord.

The devil wants us to be deceived, but Jesus came to destroy the works of the devil. "The reason the Son of God appeared was to destroy the devil's work" (1 John 3:8). We can overcome temptation because as 1 John 4:4 tells us, "The one who is in you is greater than the one who is in the world."

We have all heard the familiar song, "Tie a Yellow Ribbon 'Round the Old Oak Tree." It is the story of a boy coming home from prison. He had gotten off course, and now wondered if his loved ones would have him back. He told them he would return on a certain day on a certain bus and requested that they "tie a yellow ribbon 'round the old oak tree" if he was welcome. If the ribbon was there, he would get off the bus. If not, he would go somewhere else to start anew. When he got home he saw "a hundred yellow ribbons 'round the old oak tree."

So it is with some of us. We have wandered off course, but we are coming home to a land of beginning again. We can overcome. God has tied a ribbon around Calvary's tree to say, "I forgive you." The ribbon is red to remind us that "the blood of Jesus, his Son, purifies us from all sin" (1 John 1:7).

....

⊛ **CHAPTER THREE** ⊛

....

THE CREDIBILITY CRISIS
JAMES 1:18–27

I. True Religion Involves Knowing Christ
(James 1:18)
II. True Religion Involves Sowing Consistency
(James 1:19–25)
III. True Religion Involves Showing Character
(James 1:26–27)

Having discussed the subjects of stress and relativism, James now turns to another topic that is relevant today: the issue of true religion. Western Christianity is facing a credibility crisis.

A new phenomenon began during the "Ronald Reagan era" of the 1980s. The church stepped into the political arena and played a major role in the election of Reagan as president of the United States. Almost overnight, conservative Christianity was on the front pages of the newspapers. The church began to flex its political muscles and the temptation was to take more pride in its influence than in its spiritual power. As one might expect, the church was fighting for its reputation, integrity and credibility as the decade neared its end. Denominations continued to decline in growth, scandals were exposed in high ecclesiastical places, and immorality and extravagance have been running rampant behind the closed doors of some television ministries ever since.

The world today is longing to see true religion. There is so much counterfeit Christianity on the market today. As Eastern mysticism, radical Islamic movements and a growing secularism gather momentum and woo the younger generation through the public media and public education, it is imperative that the true church rise up and make a difference in our world until Jesus comes.

True or "pure" religion is the focus of James 1:18–27. James said that true religion is characterized by a litmus test of three important factors: knowing Christ, sowing consistency and showing character.

So many churches today are irrelevant to the felt needs of their constituents. These churches have no life, no enthusiasm and no spirit of expectancy. Yes, for many people religion is boring. In fact, it is to me! But true religion is not a religion at all. It is a vibrant, living relationship with the Lord Jesus Christ that makes a difference in our world for His sake.

How can we impact an increasingly secular society? The greatest opportunity in all of church history is before us. *Carpe Diem* — "Seize the day!" — should be the church's cry. Around us is a whole generation of baby boomers who are approaching retirement. They have bought the world's lie that people, position, possessions and power bring peace and purpose to life. And although this generation has more prosperity than any previous generation, the baby boomers have discovered that material things do not bring permanent peace or present joy. The baby boomers also outdo previous generations in such areas as divorce, drug addiction, loneliness and suicide. They are searching, grasping and looking...and we have the answers. What an opportunity we have! But how can we make a difference? By giving people a picture of what true religion is all about.

Let me repeat: Christianity is not a religion; it is a relationship. That is what differentiates Christianity from all other world religions. They are taken up with man's quest to reach God, but in Christianity God has come to man in the person of Jesus Christ. The great tragedy of religion is that it cannot change the world. The sad fact is that most of the world's wars have had their roots in religion. The hope of the western world, and the whole world for that matter, is not in religion. It is in true religion — in a personal relationship with Jesus Christ. True religion leads us to be doers of His word and not hearers only.

I. True Religion Involves Knowing Christ
James 1:18

Some scholars believe James taught a theology that is opposite to Paul's. They say the book of James is an epistle of straw that promotes a works salvation. Nothing could be further from the truth. Before James ever talked about works, he made sure we knew that salvation is in Christ alone. In James 1:18, he spoke of salvation's origin, operation and outcome.

Salvation's Origin

Biblical salvation finds its origin in a supernatural regeneration, not in works. According to James 1:18, "He [God the Father] chose to give us birth." Salvation begins with God and not with man. He chose us. Had He not done so, we would never have chosen Him. The prophet wrote, "We all, like sheep, have gone astray, each of us has turned to his own way; and the Lord has laid on him the iniquity of us all" (Isaiah 53:6).

Our salvation was preceded by an undeniable condition. As Ephesians 2:1 reminds us, "You were dead in your transgressions and sins." We were helpless and had no hope of saving ourselves.

Without Christ, we were unresponsive: "Therefore, just as sin entered the world through one man, and death through sin, and in this way death came to all men, because all sinned" (Romans 5:12). Without Christ, we were unperceptive: "And even if our gospel is veiled, it is veiled to those who are perishing..." (2 Corinthians 4:3–4). Without Christ, we were unteachable:

"The man without the Spirit does not accept the things that come from the Spirit of God, for they are foolishness to him, and he cannot understand them, because they are spiritually discerned" (1 Corinthians 2:14). Without Christ, we were unrighteous: "Surely I was sinful at birth, sinful from the time my mother conceived me" (Psalm 51:5). Such was our undeniable condition.

In the words of Jeremiah 13:23, "Can the Ethiopian change his skin or the leopard its spots? Neither can you do good who are accustomed to doing evil." Thus, if we could do nothing in and of ourselves to reach God, God had to do something. He had to take the initiative.

Our salvation was provided by an unconditional choosing. He chose to give us birth. Why do some people have trouble believing this? The same people who have no trouble believing that God called Abraham to leave Ur of the Chaldees and at the same time left all the others in Ur to follow heathenism have difficulty believing that God chooses people today. Our Lord said, "You did not choose me, but I chose you and appointed you to go and bear fruit — fruit that will last" (John 15:16). Paul put it like this: "For he chose us in him before the creation of the world to be holy and blameless in his sight" (Ephesians 1:4). And in Ephesians 2:8–10 he wrote, "For it is by grace you have been saved, through faith — and this not from yourselves, it is the gift of God — not by works, so that no one can boast. For we are God's workmanship, created in Christ Jesus to do good works, which God prepared in advance for us to do." The Bible is the continuous story of God's election.

Now, if salvation is preceded by an undeniable condition and provided by an unconditional choosing, then it logically follows that there must be some way by which God calls us to salvation. Indeed there is. Salvation is procured through an unmistakable calling. Romans 8:30 says, "Those he [God] predestined, he also called; those he called, he also justified; those he justified, he also glorified." God not only chooses to give us birth; He also calls us unto salvation.

There are two calls, the outward call and the inward call. How can two people sit on the same pew during the same church service, hear the same gospel message in the same anointing and have completely different responses? One of them may fall under deep conviction of sin, and the other may leave the room as if he had been to a movie. They both heard the outward call of the messenger, but it is the inward call to our hearts that procures our calling. Lydia is the best Biblical illustration of the inward call. "One of those listening was a woman named Lydia, a dealer in purple cloth from the city of Thyatira, who was a worshiper of God. *The Lord opened her heart* to respond to Paul's message" (Acts 16:14, *italics added*).

God chose to give us birth. This truth should intensify our evangelistic efforts. We are to preach the gospel over vale and hill to every person, to whomever will listen. No one who has not first been drawn to Christ by the Father will ever come. "No one can come to me," Jesus said, "unless the Father who sent me draws him, and I will raise him up at the last day" (John 6:44).

Yes, God birthed us. Only this new birth brings a person into real life. Education tries to turn on that light in a person, but it fails. Economics and ethics fail also. People are not getting better as evolution teaches. They are getting worse and need a spiritual birth from above.

The word translated "birth" in James 1:18 is ἀποκυέω. It means "to bring forth into being." The use of the aorist tense clearly shows that the birth is accomplished once and for all. It is a past completed action. You cannot be born again and again and again. Just as you can only be born once in the physical world, you can only be born once in the spiritual world.

John 1:13 says we are "children born not of natural descent, nor of human decision or a husband's will, but born of God." Salvation is not a result of heredity. We do not get it by osmosis. It is not brought about by persuasive preaching. The new birth is of God. Yes, true religion involves knowing Christ and knowing that salvation's origin is in God the Father.

In a day when many churches and denominations no longer believe that Jesus is the only way to Heaven, it does us good to read the reminder in James 1:18 that salvation is God's work and not ours.

   Salvation's Operation

Having discussed salvation's origin, James goes on to reveal salvation's operation by saying that God "chose to give us birth *through the word of truth*" (James 1:18, *italics added*). First Peter 1:23 puts it like this: "For you have been born again, not of perishable seed, but of imperishable, through the living and enduring word of God." No one has ever been truly converted to Christ apart from God's Word. Paul said, "Faith comes from hearing the message, and the message is heard through the word of Christ" (Romans 10:17).

There must be conviction before conversion. Only the Holy Spirit, using the Sword of the Spirit — the Word of God — upon our hearts can bring conviction. The Holy Spirit uses the Word as a hammer to break a rock to pieces (Jeremiah 23:29). The Word reveals that we are sinners and need a Savior. It also tells us the plan of salvation, how to be saved. Yes, "the word of God is living and active. Sharper than any double-edged sword, it penetrates even to dividing soul and spirit, joints and marrow; it judges the thoughts and attitudes of the heart" (Hebrews 4:12).

Salvation's operation is through the Word of Truth. No wonder so few people are being converted to Christ in so many churches in our western world. Many churches do not even teach and preach the Word of God. (Many denominations in our western culture consider the Bible to be a worn-out, antiquated book.) No wonder churches are dying. Their pastors blame the problem on location, the current culture or hundreds of other things, but the fact is there is no salvation apart from the Word of God. This is why it is imperative to have teachers in seminaries who believe the Bible is the infallible and inerrant Word of God.

The Word of God, living and written, is God's instrument of salvation. This is why few people are converted in liberal churches where the Bible is not preached. True religion involves knowing Christ, knowing that salvation has its origin in the sovereignty of God and knowing that salvation operates through the Word of God.

Salvation's Outcome

Having shared with us salvation's origin and operation, James continues to reveal salvation's outcome: "That we might be a kind of firstfruits of all he created" (James 1:18). The Word of God is the seed that brings forth fruit (1 Peter 1:23).

Our Lord was referring to this truth when He said, "Unless a kernel of wheat falls to the ground and dies, it remains only a single seed. But if it dies, it produces many seeds" (John 12:24). Jesus says that life comes from death, though the natural man says, "No, that is absurd. Death comes from life."

Imagine that you have a grain of wheat in your hand. Drop it into the earth. Cover it over. Let it die. That little grain corrodes and rots and then releases its life germ. After a little while, a tiny blade pushes its way through the soil and reaches up toward the sun. Days and weeks pass, and the blade eventually becomes a full-grown plant that produces hundreds of little seeds like the one you planted. All of that was in the little grain of wheat, but you could not see it. Until the tiny grain of wheat died, it could not have life. But then it produced many other little grains just like itself — many other "first fruits."

Now imagine that instead of planting that little grain of wheat, you drop it in your desk drawer. You leave it there for six months and then go back to the drawer and open it. The seed is still there, abiding alone.

During His days on earth, Jesus remained just like that little grain in the drawer. He produced nothing exactly like Himself. Even the disciples argued over who would be the greatest in His kingdom. On the night when He needed them the most, they forsook Him and fled. But what a difference when Jesus died, was planted in the earth and then came forth! No longer did He abide alone. He became the "firstborn among many brothers" (Romans 8:29).

The first-century Christians to whom James addressed his letter were the first generation to trust in the Lord Jesus Christ as their promised Messiah. James called them the "firstfruits" in God's new family (James 1:18).

Once a person becomes a part of God's family, he, too, will bear fruit. Our Lord says, "By their fruit you will recognize them" (Matthew 7:16). Since fruit is the outcome of salvation, fruit is a sign that we know Christ. Knowing Christ is the beginning of true religion.

II. True Religion Involves Sowing Consistency
James 1:19–25

True religion involves knowing Christ and sowing consistency. Consistency manifests itself in two ways: in our talk and in our walk. If we are to present the world with a true picture of Christ, then we must not only know Him; we must also be consistent in our talk and our walk. Sadly, many believers' talk and walk do not lineup. Their conversation and conduct are at odds. They say one thing and do another.

Consistent in Talk

One of the true marks of genuine Christianity is a person's consistency in conversation. James 1:19–21 reveals to us the importance of what we say and how we listen. James 1:19 says we should be "quick to listen." Jesus says it this way: "He who has ears, let him hear" (Matthew 13:9). One reason there are so many broken relationships is that people stop listening to each other. Communication can break down between husbands and wives, between parents and children, and between employers and employees. Consistency in talk means that we listen more than we speak.

James 1:19 goes on to say that we should be "slow to speak." It doesn't say that we should not speak, but that we should think before we speak. It is no coincidence that we each have two ears and one mouth. Could it be that we should listen twice as much as we talk?

Some of us reverse the admonition of Scripture; we are slow to listen and quick to speak. And that often is the reason we get into trouble. Some of us would rather talk than listen. When we meet people, we give the standard greeting, "How are you?" They tell us, but usually we do not listen. Why? We are concentrating on telling them something about ourselves. When we are introduced to someone, we cannot even recall the person's name five seconds later. Why? We do not listen. Instead of being quick to listen and slow to speak, so many of us are just the opposite.

Solomon, the wisest man who ever lived, said, "When words are many, sin is not absent, but he who holds his tongue is wise ...A man of knowledge uses words with restraint, and a man of understanding is even-tempered" (Proverbs 10:19;17:27). Jesus warns that "men will have to give account on the day of judgment for every careless word they have spoken. For by your words you will be acquitted, and by your words you will be condemned" (Matthew 12:36–37).

The tongue can be a dangerous weapon. Some use it for blasting. They gossip. Some use it for boasting. Others use it for blistering. Isn't it strange how some people build themselves up by tearing others down? Many Christians who would never think of physically abusing their spouses verbally abuse them day and night. The tongue is not to be used for blasting, boasting or blistering; it is to be used for blessing.

James 1:19 also says that we are to be "slow to become angry." It does not say that we are not to become angry, but that we are to be slow in doing so. We are to have a godly anger against sin. Paul said, "In your anger do not sin" (Ephesians 4:26).

After cautioning us about our speech and our anger, James revealed what we should do with our sin. He said, "Get rid of all moral filth and the evil that is so prevalent and humbly accept the word planted in you, which can save you" (James 1:21). The Greek word translated "Get rid of," ἀποτίθημι, means "to put off, to strip away." The word could be used to describe someone taking off a coat. Thus it is our responsibility to strip off all moral filth. Although God has called us and chosen us, there is still something for us to do. We must take off our old coats of sin.

We do not take off our sins in order to be saved, since only the blood of Christ can take our sins away. James was writing to Christians who already know Christ (James 1:18). Since they know Christ, they should sow consistency in their talk and walk.

They know better. Therefore James was saying, "Stop sinning. Get rid of those old coats of moral filth."

Why is it that some people can't seem to get rid of their sin? A joke I heard my cousin tell when I was a little child will help explain the reason. The corny story is about a man who saw another man walking down the street. He stopped him and said, "Mister, you have a banana in your ear."

"What?" replied the second man.

"You have a banana in your ear."

The statement and response went back and forth several times until finally the second man replied, "I am sorry I can't hear you. I have a banana in my ear."

God is telling some people today, "You have sin in your life. Get rid of it." But they can't hear Him. Why? Because they have sin in their lives.

The Greek word ῥυπαρία is translated "moral filth" in James 1:21 and "shabby clothes" in James 2:2. This word is, in fact, a compound word from which we get the words "ear wax," the liquid secretion that keeps insects and debris from penetrating the ear. James was using this word picture to drive home the truth that filth in our lives will keep us from hearing the Word of God. Sin in our lives, like too much wax in our ears, prevents the Word of Truth from reaching our hearts.[1]

Not many preachers preach hard on sin today. An oft-repeated story is about a group of deacons who complained to their preacher that he was preaching too plainly about sin. "The boys, girls and teenagers," they said, "are hearing too much about sin, and it might make it easier for them to become sinners."

The minister took out a bottle of strychnine that was marked poison on the label. "Is this what you want me to do?" the pastor asked, removing the label. "Do you want me to change the label and put on the bottle the words spirit of peppermint?"

The milder we make the label, the more dangerous the poison becomes. James called sin what it is — moral filth and evil — and he called on us to throw it off like a dirty old coat. Too many preachers in our modern age never mention the word sin, but James did not back off from it. Nor should we. Sin wrecks everything it touches. We need to get rid of the sin and inconsistencies in our talk.

Consistent in Walk

James went on to reveal how important it is for us to be consistent in our walk. He said, "Do not merely listen to the word, and so deceive yourselves. Do what it says. Anyone who listens to the word but does not do what it says is like a man who looks at his face in a mirror and, after looking at himself, goes away and immediately forgets what he looks like. But the man who looks intently into the perfect law that gives freedom, and continues to do this, not forgetting what he has heard, but doing it — he will be blessed in what he does" (James 1:22–25).

Blessing does not come by simply hearing great biblical truths. It is not the hearing, but the doing that produces blessing. James said, "He will be blessed in what he does." The question is, What are we doing about what we are hearing? It is better to do one sermon than hear a thousand sermons.

How did you learn to ride a bicycle? Did you read the manual? Did you learn by watching others? Did you learn by listening to your dad tell you how to try to keep your balance? No. You did not learn to ride your bicycle until you got on it and tried — until you did it.

How do we learn to play the piano? By listening to the teacher play? By reading the sheet music? No. We learn by pounding out the notes, by practicing the music over and over again.

The word "do" in James 1:22 is a translation of the interesting Greek word ποιητής. The noun form is ποιημα, from which we get our word "poet." A poet is creative; he puts words together in order to express a thought or meaning. Ποιητής does not simply mean to be busy with activities. It is a word of creativity.

The word "listen" in James 1:22 is a translation of the Greek word ἀκροατής, which literally means "audit." The word reminds us of a person auditing a college course. He attends the classes, hears all the lectures, but never has to take the tests. He doesn't receive a grade. When exam time comes, he can go to the beach while others study. When term papers are due, he can go away for a weekend while others cram. There is absolutely no pressure. However, when graduation comes and the diplomas are handed out, there is no cap and gown or diploma for the student who has only audited courses. Many church members are just hearers; that is, they just audit the course. They don't visit others in need. They don't keep unspotted from the world. They don't work in a Bible study department. They are not involved in evangelism training. They don't come to Bible studies. They don't return a tithe to the Lord. They have heard all the teaching and they believe it, but they just never get the grade. Where will they be on graduation day?

These people tragically "deceive themselves" (James 1:22). "Deceive" is derived from παραλογίζομαι. This Greek word, an accounting term, means "to cheat yourself," to miscalculate a figure in a ledger. When a grocery clerk gives you the wrong change, or a contractor offers to do work on your home and rips you off, you don't like it. You hate it when someone else deceives you. So why should you cheat yourself? Yet the Bible says if you hear the Word and never do it, you are simply deceiving yourself.

James compared the person who merely listens to someone who looks in a mirror. The Greek word for "look" in James 1:23

means a casual, haphazard glance. James had in mind a fellow who walks by and glances at himself in a mirror. He looks, but he goes away and forgets what he has seen (1:24). The parallel to people today is all too clear. A Christian comes to the Bible, glances at it hurriedly, skims over a passage and hears what he ought to do. He bows his head for a quick prayer and then runs off to his business meeting. An hour later he has forgotten what he read.

Have you ever found yourself described in these verses? If you adhere to an easy believism — you only hear and have no fruit, you never do what the Word says — you deceive yourself. Paul wrote, "Do not be deceived: God cannot be mocked. A man reaps what he sows" (Galatians 6:7).

Now it is vitally important to know God's Word, but how much more important it is to obey it — to do it. I like to eat out, but I do not gain nourishment by staring at the menu. The chef does not make barbecue sauce by staring at the recipe. Builders do not construct skyscrapers by staring at the blueprints. Why do some of us think the Christian life is different? Why do some of us think we can please Christ by staring at the blueprint, the recipe or the menu? We must do what the Bible says. Jesus said, "Whoever has my commands and obeys them, he is the one who loves me" (John 14:21). He also said, "My mother and brothers are those who hear God's word and put it into practice" (Luke 8:21).

While salvation is spelled d-o-n-e and is completely provided for us in Christ, our actions are pretty good proof that we are truly saved. First John 2:3–6 says: "We know that we have come to know him if we obey his commands. The man who says, 'I know him,' but does not do what he commands is a liar, and the truth is not in him. But if anyone obeys his word, God's love is truly made complete in him. This is how we know we are in him: Whoever claims to live in him must walk as Jesus did." We must sow consistency in our walk.

James likened the Bible to a mirror. It shows us what we are really like. Sometimes, even when a friend looks haggard, you might respond politely, "Oh, you look great!" But the mirror tells the truth. Think about it. Many beautiful women are glad their mirrors cannot tell others what they look like first thing in the morning: the puffy eyes, the blotched complexions, the pale faces, the dry lips and the disheveled hair. We own mirrors in order to see what we really look like. The Bible is like a mirror. We can look into it and see our spiritual condition. The Word of God gives us an accurate reflection of ourselves and shows us what we are really like in God's eyes, not what we think we are or what others say we are.

The Bible shows us what we are without all our pretenses and cover-ups. We seldom look at ourselves in a mirror in the morning without doing something about our appearance. Nor should we just hear the Word without acting on it. Looking into the mirror of God's Word should make us want to "do it." Merely listening to the Word without doing what it says is self-deception.

Job saw himself as he really was and said: "My ears had heard of you but now my eyes have seen you. Therefore I despise myself and repent in dust and ashes" (Job 42:5–6). Isaiah had a vision of the holiness of God and said: "Woe to me!…I am ruined! For I am a man of unclean lips, and I live among a people of unclean lips, and my eyes have seen the King, the Lord Almighty" (Isaiah 6:5). Peter looked at the Living Word, saw himself as he really was and said, "Go away from me, Lord; I am a sinful man" (Luke 5:8).

Have you looked at yourself in the mirror of the Bible lately? Oh, I'm not talking about a passing glance. Stay there for a moment. Look at yourself through the mirror of Psalm 51 or Psalm 139. Take a good look. See yourself in these words: "Search me, O God, and know my heart; test me and know my anxious thoughts. See if there is any offensive way in me, and lead me in the way everlasting" (Psalm 139:23–24).

If you stand long enough in front of the mirror of God's Word, you will see yourself as a sinner who has no hope of satisfying the righteous demands of the law in and of yourself. You will see that you need a Savior, and you will bow before Him. Do you know why many people do not seek Christ? They are not aware of their sin. They are self-deceived. They have never looked into the mirror of the Word. Remember, "He chose to give us birth through the *word of truth*" (James 1:18, *italics added*).

James 1:25 talks about a man who "looks intently into the perfect law that gives freedom." The words translated "looks intently" come from the Greek word παρακύπτω, which means "to stoop down and look intently in order to see something." This look is not just a casual glance. It is the studied look of someone who bends over a mirror in order to examine a feature more intently.[2] We are to look intently into the Word of God, which is our mirror.

Παρακύπτω is different from κατανοέω, which was used in James 1:23–24 to mean simply "a glance." Παρακύπτω speaks of a real commitment. We find this same word in John 20:5: "He bent over and looked in at the strips of linen lying there but did not go in." It is also found in John 20:11: "Mary stood outside the tomb crying. As she wept, she bent over to look into the tomb." John and Mary stooped and looked into the empty tomb, studying it carefully. They looked carefully and intently with the full attention of their hearts and souls. Just as they looked intently into the empty tomb, we are to look intently into the Bible. Some of us stand before the mirror at home for 30 minutes at a time. If we looked intently into the Bible for 30 minutes, we would be more spiritually pleasing to God.

The man in James 1:25 continues to look intently into the Bible. "Continue" is a translation of the Greek word παραμένω, which means "to stay on course." This man doesn't just begin and then turn aside. Every day he opens the mirror of the Word and looks intently therein. As a result of staying on course, he will be blessed. The use of an emphatic in the original language of this verse means that this man, and this man alone, will be blessed.

Note how he is blessed. James 1:25 says, "in what he does." Jesus said, "Now that you know these things, you will be blessed *if* you do them" (John 13:17, *italics added*). People are not blessed by Christianity if they do not practice what the Bible teaches. The blessing comes not in the knowledge of great Biblical truth, but in the practicing — the doing — of it. There is no joy in knowing the truth about tithing and not doing it. But there is tremendous joy in being a steward of God-given resources. Spiritual blessing comes not in knowing God's truth, but in practicing it.

Some people think blessing comes from being a "super-spiritual sponge." Have you ever known people who were just "too spiritual" to do the work of ministry? They form little holy huddles and go deeper and deeper into the Word, but they are hearers only. They are simply auditing the course. They forget that we are equipped for the work of the ministry. Churches that are free of fusses, fightings and splits are blessed because of what they do. When people are involved in doing, they have little time to break fellowship with others.

How can we sow consistency in our talk and walk? By accepting the Word (James 1:21). There is a subtle danger for the believer who avidly reads books about the Bible while neglecting the Bible itself. Beware of this. The Word is what is quickened to us by the Holy Spirit. He is our primary teacher, and the Bible is our spiritual mirror.

James says we are to "accept" the Word. Δέχομαι, the Greek word translated "accept" in James 1:21, means "to accept or receive as the door by which we enter." We are not saved by working, but by receiving. We are saved not by what we can give to God, but by what He gives to us. We accept His free gift. If we do not accept this Word by faith, it cannot bless us. We do not judge it; it judges us. It is important to note that this Greek word is an aorist imperative. It means once and for all. It is already done.

James 1:21 says to approach the Bible "humbly" (πραΰτης). This is the same word translated in the Beatitudes as "meek" (Matthew 5:5). In classical Greek, πραΰτης is used to describe an animal that has been domesticated — for example, a wild stallion who has come under the control of a master. The horse's will has been broken; he is powerful, but he is obedient. We are to come under the control of the Word and accept it with humility and meekness. We are to bend before the lordship of Christ. Many do not accept the Word because they will not come under the control of the Master.

We are enabled to accept the Word humbly because it is "planted" (ἔμφυτος) within us (James 1:21). The Greek word is translated in the King James Version as "engrafted." Charles Spurgeon saw in this verse the picture of a graft on a tree. When a limb is to be grafted into a tree, the first step is to make two gashes or cuts: one in the tree and the other in the limb. It is a blessed thing when the wounded Savior connects with a wounded heart. No one has ever genuinely accepted the Word who has not first been wounded by its truth. When people heard the Word of God at Pentecost, their hearts were cut (Acts 2:37). Their hearts were opened and the living Word was placed within. When the Word is accepted in meekness, the living limb begins to receive its strength from the sap of the tree. They begin to grow into one another. Jesus said, "If you remain in me and my words remain in you…" (John 15:7). When the limb and the tree grow into each other, fruit is produced.

Most likely, however, the word "planted" is a better translation than "engrafted." James was not telling us to accept this Word for the first time, since it has already been planted there.[3] Probably James had Christ's parable of the sower and the seed in mind (Matthew 13:1–23). In this parable Jesus compared God's Word to seed and the human heart to soil. Some of the soil was fertile. It accepted the seed. When we humbly accept the planted Word, it is able to save us (James 1:21). The word save means "to carry on to the end." James was not speaking of an initial salvation experience, but of deliverance.

True Christians who humbly accept the planted Word can become not only hearers, but doers of God's Word. True religion involves knowing Christ, sowing consistency in talk and walk and showing character.

III. True Religion Involves Showing Character
James 1:26-27

There is a lot of counterfeit Christianity in our day. James 1:26 says, "If anyone considers himself religious..." Many people consider themselves to be religious. However, their Christianity could be compared to an ecclesiastical cafeteria. They think they can go through the Bible and pick and choose which commands to obey like they pick food in a cafeteria line. The Bible says, "Don't be disobedient to your parents." Someone likes that one and puts it on his tray. The Bible also says "Don't commit adultery," but he just passes that one by and leaves it on the shelf. And the tragedy is, such people consider themselves to be religious.

But it is a sham. In fact, the Lord said, "Not everyone who says to me 'Lord, Lord,' will enter the kingdom of heaven, but only he who does the will of my Father who is in heaven. Many will say to me on that day, 'Lord, Lord, did we not prophesy in your name, and in your name drive out demons and perform many miracles?' Then I will tell them plainly 'I never knew you'"

(Matthew 7:21–23). John put it like this: "They went out from us, but they did not really belong to us. For if they had belonged to us, they would have remained with us; but their going showed that none of them belonged to us" (1 John 2:19).

They were counterfeits. How are genuine Christians different? True believers not only know Christ and sow consistency; they also show character. Christian character is evidenced in three ways: by conversation, by concern and by conduct.

The Evidence of Our Conversation

Our Christian character is evidenced by our conversation. James 1:26 says, "If anyone considers himself religious and yet does not keep a tight rein on his tongue, he deceives himself and his religion is worthless." Two things happen when one does not control his tongue: he deceives himself; and his religion is worthless. It is an empty show.

The word translated "deceives" is the Greek ἀπατάω. It also means "cheats." If we don't control our tongues, we tragically cheat ourselves out of joy and happiness.

The word translated "worthless" is the Greek μάταιος, which means "without achieving its intended result or goal."[4] A worthless religion is of no value whatever; it is futile, fruitless. Words and actions that do not spring from faith are worthless. They will one day be burned up, as Paul said in 1 Corinthians 3:12–15.

The Evidence of Our Concern

True religion is demonstrated by our character, and our character is evidenced not only by conversation, but also by concern. James 1:27 says, "Religion that God our Father accepts as pure and faultless is this: to look after orphans and widows."

Did James mean that if we just pay some folks a visit everything will be all right? No. He was simply using as examples two of the most obvious recipients of our concern — orphans and widows. In the first century, there were no insurance policies or Social Security benefits. When the breadwinner died, trouble knocked at the door. Orphans became victims of the street, often abused by perverts and traded by slave owners. Widows had no social standing. Many had to turn to immorality to provide for themselves. James was saying that we are to be concerned about those who are suffering and sorrowful and those who need to be protected and cared for. We are to show mercy to those who cannot reciprocate.

James was not saying we are saved by these good works. No one should misunderstand this. Being saved never results from good works, but being saved does result in good works. Paul reminded us that we are "created in Christ Jesus to do good works" (Ephesians 2:10).

The Greek word translated "look after" in James 1:27 (NIV) or "visit" in the King James Version is ἐπισκέπτομαι, which means "to see or to inspect."[5] It is a compound of a preposition that means "over" and another word that means "to look after."[6] Επισκέπτομαι literally means "to care for." It is properly translated in the NIV because it means so much more than a simple visit. In fact, ἐπισκέπτομαι is the root of our word "bishop," which means "overseer." James was not urging us to pay casual visits to orphans and widows. He was telling us to demonstrate deep spiritual concern for anyone who is in need. The duty of every Christian is to serve others. The service that results from concern is one of the most obvious marks of true Christian character.

The Evidence of Our Conduct

James completes his first chapter by saying, "Keep oneself from being polluted by the world" (James 1:27). Too many Christians are polluted by the world — the κόσμος — the world system. They think and act in accordance with the value systems of our society instead of the value systems of the Word of God.

My wife often shops at a local clearance center not far from our home. Everything is marked down 50% or more. (She keeps telling me how much money she saves by shopping there so often!) One time there was a big table heaped with all sorts of odds and ends — shirts, pants, sweaters and the like. The sign on that table read something to this effect: "Slightly soiled — greatly reduced in price." How those words penetrated my heart. Think about them. "Slightly soiled — greatly reduced in price." How many Christians have had those words written on their lives? Christians whose lives are spotted and stained by sin lose so much of the value of the Christian life.

There are decisions that you and I must make to keep ourselves unpolluted. We should, for instance, stay away from compromising situations. The tense of the Greek verb meaning "unpolluted" indicates that we are to keep on keeping ourselves unspotted.

James was not saying that we are to stay out of the world and assume monk-like isolation. No, James was talking insulation here, not isolation. Jesus says that we are to be in the world but not of the world (John 17:14–16). We are to be the salt of what? The church? No. The earth. We are to be the light of what? The church? No. The world. (See Matthew 5:13–14.) We are to penetrate a secular society with the message of Christ. Jesus didn't die on a gold cross on a mahogany communion table in a carpeted, air-conditioned church. He died in a world where men were sweating, cursing and gambling, and that is exactly where he told us to take the gospel.

How can we be insulated as we take this message to the world? First by knowing Christ, then by sowing consistency, and finally by showing character.

One of the great issues facing the church as we enter the third millennium is the credibility crisis. Are we credible? Are we living a lie, or are we living a Christlike life? The world is watching and waiting to see if we are real.

To be credible we must do what the Bible says. We can never earn salvation by doing what the Bible says about conversation and conduct, but because we are saved, we will want to bridle our tongues, show concern for others and lead pure lives before God.

Our Lord ended the greatest sermon ever preached with a message about the importance of doing what the Word of God says. He told the story of two men who built identical homes. When the homes were constructed, everything looked the same from the outside...until the storm came. The winds blew, the rain pelted upon the houses, and one of the houses fell flat while the other stood firm. The house that stood firm was built on solid rock. Jesus revealed that its builder is a picture of someone "who hears these words of mine and puts them into practice" (Matthew 7:24).

....

⊛ **CHAPTER FOUR** ⊛

....

DISCRIMINATION
JAMES 2:1-13

1. The False Leg of Prejudice (James 2:1-7)
II. The False Leg of Presumption (James 2:8-13)

During the last years of the twentieth century, some major changes swept across our world. In the former Soviet Union, Jews who have been discriminated against for scores of years were being freed in growing numbers for emigration to Israel. The Berlin wall crumbled. Eastern Europe taught us that no one can be suppressed and discriminated against indefinitely. In South Africa, change continues to be in the wind; the day has come when racial equality exists in that strife-filled land. (Does that sound strange? We in America must remember that we are only my own generation removed from racial segregation.)

Yet in the Middle East discrimination is at an all-time high as Arab and Jewish conflict intensifies with each passing year. And in the United States there still remain pockets of racial discrimination between black and white, Jew and Gentile.

Ironically, one victim of intense discrimination in the western world is conservative Christianity. Anti-Christian bigotry is accelerating at a rapid pace. Christmas carols are no longer allowed in many schools. Nativity scenes are removed from town squares. The Motion Picture Association of America gave the Billy Graham film *The Prodigal* a "parental guidance" rating. Why? Because, according to the M.P.A.A., "Pre-teenage children should not be exposed to Christianity without their parents' consent." Strange, isn't it, that young people can get abortions without parental consent, but they cannot be exposed to

Christianity without it? A federal court ruled that the seal of Bernalillo County, New Mexico, was illegal. Why? The seal, which was established when the county was formed, consisted of a mountain range, grazing sheep and a cross suspended in the sky. In Fort Lauderdale, Florida, a teacher was reprimanded for showing a film on creationism to a biology class. A principal in DeKalb County, Georgia, suspended a sophomore for "possession of Christian literature" (an invitation to a Fellowship of Christian Athletes meeting). His father met with the principal, who informed him that the boy could not carry a pocket New Testament to school either. The enraged parents filed a lawsuit against the school district.

Anti-Christian bigotry is on the rise. One reason is that secularists know that Christians generally "turn the other cheek" and do not fight back like Jewish people with their Anti-Defamation League, or blacks with their National Association for the Advancement of Colored People, or liberals with their American Civil Liberties Union. It is time for the church to take the issue of discrimination more seriously.

The church must not avoid the issue of discrimination from without — or discrimination within. One would think after more than 2,000 years of church history that James 2:1–13 would be irrelevant. Unfortunately, these verses are still extremely poignant.

The church of the Lord Jesus ought to be one place where discrimination is a dirty word. But not so! I am amazed at how few sermons can be found on the subject of discrimination in the church. Have you noticed how in some churches the congregation looks like they were all made from the same cookie cutter? They all look the same, dress the same, talk the same and have the same hairstyle. They come from the same economic and social levels.

There are all kinds of subtle discrimination within the church. There is discrimination on the basis of race. Some people discriminate against blacks, whites or Hispanics. Others discriminate on the basis of resources and have nothing to do with anyone who is not on their economic level. Some have no respect for others unless they are of the same social class or of the same sex.

Discrimination can work both ways. Christians with money discriminate against those without it. Christians without money discriminate against those who have money and respond with jealousy, envy and suspicion. I know whites who discriminate against blacks and I know blacks who discriminate against whites. The same is true with Jews and Gentiles.

One of my fondest childhood memories was a trip to the circus at the old Will Rogers Coliseum in Fort Worth, Texas. I was particularly intrigued by a certain clown act. One of the clowns stood about eight feet tall. He was really not that tall. The truth is he was walking around on stilts and had long pants covering them. His partner was about three feet tall. These two clowns carried on in such a fashion that the whole audience was soon laughing uproariously. The tall man got the best of the short man until the final part of their act. Then the little person sneaked up behind the tall man and knocked the stilts out from under him, and he became a little person also. I tell that story to make a point. Discrimination — a cursed, dirty sin — stands on two stilts, two false legs that need to be knocked out from under it. One false leg is prejudice and the other is presumption. The intent of this chapter is to knock these false legs out from under this enemy of the cross.

I. The False Leg of Prejudice
James 2:1–7

An Explanation

· What is prejudice? It is defined as "bias because of a fixed idea; an opinion arrived at without taking time and care to judge fairly." Mark Twain said, "Prejudice is the ink with which all history is written."[1] Many wars and major world conflicts have been the direct result of prejudicial thinking. Prejudice is one of the stilts on which discrimination stands.

James was firmly opposed to prejudice. He said, "Don't show favoritism" (James 2:1). The Greek word for "favoritism," προσωπολημψία, literally means "to lay hold of one's face," that is, to judge by how one appears to be on the outside. For example, when someone wears a certain type of jewelry or clothes, it is easy to make a judgment based on what we see on the outside. But James was saying, "Don't do this. Do not show favoritism. Do not just look at the outward appearance."

Prejudice can work both ways. While some people show favoritism to the rich and forget the outcasts, others show favoritism to the outcasts to the exclusion and disdain of the rich. Some are partial to the "haves" while others are partial to the "have-nots."[2]

Prejudice is not just prevalent in politics, business and social circles. It has found its way into many churches, too. James' warning is particularly pertinent for churches. Remember, the Lord Jesus did not look on the outward appearance; He looked on the heart. He was not impressed by how many possessions people had, who they knew, how high they had climbed up the social ladder or how many times their pictures had appeared on the society page. He had as much respect for the poor widow as

He did for wealthy Joseph of Arimathaea. Jesus was known for His compassion, not for compromise.

The people to whom James addressed his letter seemed to be flattering the rich in hopes of getting something from them. One wise old sage explained the difference between gossip and flattery: Gossip is what we say behind someone's back that we would never say to his face; flattery is what we say to someone's face that we would never say behind his back. When a flatterer sees someone he hasn't seen in quite a while, he says to her face, "Oh, you look so young." After she leaves, he turns to a friend and says, "Isn't she looking old?"[3]

James was saying, "Stop it! Do not show favoritism." We are to be like the Lord Jesus who looked on the heart. We are to love the rich and the outcasts alike. Whenever the church meets, everyone should be equal. No person in any fellowship is one bit better than any of the others. Prejudice in the Christian faith has no leg upon which to stand.

An Illustration

James 2:2–4 illustrates this truth: "Suppose a man comes into your meeting wearing a gold ring and fine clothes, and a poor man in shabby clothes also comes in. If you show special attention to the man wearing fine clothes and say, 'Here's a good seat for you,' but say to the poor man, 'You stand there' or 'Sit on the floor by my feet,' have you not discriminated among yourselves and become judges with evil thoughts?"

Do you get the picture? A worship service is about to start. In walk two men. One is wearing a $2,000 designer suit, a gold watch and a gold ring; the other comes in wearing clothes from the clothing ministry room. A certain usher, enamored with outward appearance, escorts the rich man to the best seat and says to the poor man, "Go stand over there, out of the way." The real problem here is not in finding a seat for the rich man, but in ignoring the poor man. We must remember the words of 1 Samuel 16:7: "The Lord does not look at the things man looks at. Man looks at the outward appearance, but the Lord looks at the heart."

At this point many people try to make the Scriptures say something they are not saying. There's nothing wrong with wearing a gold ring or a gold watch. James was dealing with an issue far deeper than that. Gold rings were marks of social status in the first century. The man in James' story was wearing what he was wearing in order to draw attention to himself. It was his way of trying to be recognized and given a prominent seat. He was like the scribes and Pharisees whom our Lord rebuked: "They love the place of honor at banquets and the most important seats in the synagogues" (Matthew 23:6).

While I was pastoring in Fort Lauderdale, two men died whom God used to touch my life in special ways. One was a wealthy man by the world's standards, probably a millionaire. For a generation he had been one of the backbones of our church. He sat about halfway back in the auditorium and never missed a service. He never pushed himself into leadership, but did more to help our church and people than any other man I have ever known. Time and again when I heard of a family struggling, I would call him and he would anonymously give money for rent or other emergencies. He used his contacts to help untold numbers of people find jobs. He was one of the greatest friends I have ever had, and I miss him very much.

The other man lived in an institutional retirement center not far from downtown Fort Lauderdale. His pants were about two sizes too big and the cuffs were rolled halfway up his calves so that his sockless feet and worn tennis shoes showed. His shirt was usually buttoned in the wrong holes, and there he would sit every Sunday morning on the front row. Only Heaven has recorded how many times I looked down into his face and breathed a prayer of thanksgiving to God for that man's presence. It constantly reminded me, as the preacher and pastor, of how welcome the outcasts of society should be in God's house.

We must be careful not to confuse the issue here. There is nothing wrong with wealth. "The *love of money*," not money, "is a root of all kinds of evil" (1 Timothy 6:10, *italics added*). Some people who have very little money love it more than some who are wealthy. It is not sinful to be rich, and it is not spiritual to be poor. There are many rich people who are spiritual, and many poor people who are sinful.

Another subtle danger in many churches, especially in times of financial crisis, is to cater to people who can help the church rather than to people the church can help. We ought to always fight this attitude. God has a way of taking care of everything else when we keep our priorities in order.

Discrimination has no place in the church of the Lord Jesus. It stands on a shaky leg of prejudice, and James accused his readers of being guilty of this sin.

An Accusation

James began his accusation by saying, "Listen, my dear brothers" (James 2:5). He was teaching us the important lesson that when we confront our Christian brothers and sisters with their sins, we should always do so in love. Before he made the accusation he wanted his brothers in Christ to know he loved them and was confronting them for their good and for God's glory.

The accusation is stinging: "You have insulted the poor" (James 2:6). The word for "insult," ἀτιμάζω, is an aorist active verb that means "to treat without honor, to dishonor — to take away one's dignity." If a poor man enters the house of God and receives discrimination instead of respect as a human being or a child of God, the last precious thing he possesses has been taken from him: his dignity and honor. We must guard against insulting anyone. Why? Because Jesus said, "Whatever you did for one of the least of these brothers of mine, you did for me" (Matthew 25:40). James was saying, "Don't deny their dignity; don't steal their honor."

James 2:5 asks, "Has not God chosen those who are poor in the eyes of the world to be rich in faith and to inherit the kingdom he promised those who love him?" Don't make the mistake of thinking that poverty makes a person one of God's favorites. That idea leads to a perverted kind of pride among the poor. The Greek word for "poor," πτωχός, means "to crouch or cower with fear."[4] James had in mind the kind of man who is humble in the presence of others and particularly in the presence of God. Those of us who have humbled ourselves and by faith trusted in the finished work of Christ on the cross are the ones who inherit the kingdom. The Greek word for "inherit," κληρονόμος, means "to possess or to get ahold of." Those who love Christ have gotten hold of and possessed their inheritance.

Why is it that the poor seem to grasp the gospel in greater numbers than the rich and powerful? Is it because Christianity is not a thinking man's religion? No. In general, the poor are more aware of their powerlessness and it is easier for them to acknowledge their need of salvation. Often the rich and powerful see no need of Christ. The greatest barrier to reaching them with the gospel is their pride and boasting, while the greatest barrier to reaching the poor with the gospel is often their self-pity and bitterness.

James 2:6 says that the rich "exploit" (καταδυναστεύω) others. In Greek the word literally means "pressed down or to rule or to have power over." This strong word is used only one other time in all of Scripture. It is found in Acts 10:38 where reference is made to those who were "under the power of the devil." James was saying that we should all wake up and realize that the rich people we may be catering to are the very people who will exercise their power to bear down on us. He was saying that rich people can be ruthless oppressors.

James was accusing his readers of giving rich people places of honor while pushing back into the corner the very people among whom Jesus spent His entire earthly ministry. It is a strong accusation, not a simple insinuation.

Jesus developed special relationships with the poor. He was born in the most impoverished circumstances imaginable. When He was dedicated in the temple, His parents could only afford two turtle doves. In His first sermon, He read from Isaiah: "The Spirit of the Lord is on me, because he has anointed me to preach good news to the poor" (Luke 4:18).

The more we become like Jesus, the more we will show mercy to the poor and rejected people of society, and the less we will "insult the poor." Jesus loves needy people. If only one institution in the world goes door to door seeking a bunch of poverty-stricken people who the world says will be liabilities instead of assets, it ought to be the New Testament church.

When our Lord went to Jerusalem, He did not show favoritism. He talked to an invalid at the pool of Bethesda and also to Nicodemus, a ruler of the Jews. When Jesus went through Jericho, He did not show favoritism. He called to rich Zacchaeus who was hiding in the tree, and He healed blind Bartimaeus who was begging by the roadside. Some churches today ignore the outcasts while other churches ignore the rich. But James said, "Do not show favoritism."

I love the sign that D. L. Moody placed over the door of his church in Chicago: "Ever welcome to this house of God are the strangers and the poor." Does this mean we should ignore the upper classes? No, we are to preach the gospel to every person. But we are never to neglect anyone, regardless of race, resources or respectability. Quite frankly, if there is a segment of western society that the church has neglected, it is not the poor, but the rich. Jesus loved them all, just the same.

One reason the early church grew so rapidly was that prejudice was laid aside. Although the Jews and Samaritans hated each other, there was a place for Nicodemus, a ruler of the Jews, and a place for the woman of Samaria, who was formerly the town prostitute. In that early church there was a place for Onesimus, the former slave, and one for Philemon, his former master. Wealthy Barnabas gave a large parcel of real estate to the missionary church at Antioch, and alongside him was a place for a blind beggar who rattled a tin cup on the side streets of Jericho. The gospel gives everyone a place of dignity.

The vile sin of discrimination stands on two false legs that must be knocked from under it. One of those, as we've seen, is prejudice. The other is presumption.

II. The False Leg of Presumption
James 2:8–13

Those who discriminate are presumptuous. They presume three things: that discrimination is not sin, is not significant and is not serious.

Presumption Number One: Discrimination Is Not Sin

Some people believe that discrimination is simply a way of life. How many times have we heard, "Well, I'm from the state of _____ and that's just the way things are over there."

They falsely presume that God is just smiling and saying, "O yes, I know how it is." But in God's eyes that excuse is not cute; it is ugly. Discrimination is sin. To presume otherwise is to make a false presumption.

James 2:9 says, "If you show favoritism, you sin and are convicted by the law as lawbreakers." The Greek word for "lawbreaker," παραβάτης, refers to a man who has a prescribed course to walk, but steps over the line and walks beside the intended path instead of on it; he deviates from God's intended course. When we discriminate and presume that we are not sinning, we step over the line as far as God is concerned. The Bible calls discrimination sin. God is as serious about the sin of prejudice as He is about the sin of perversion.

What should we do when we commit the sin of discrimination? Some say we should start trying to like or love the one against whom we discriminated. No! We should deal with discrimination as we would any other sin. We confess it to God and then forsake it.

James said that we are to abide by what he called the "royal law," which is to "love your neighbor as yourself" (James 2:8). The Lord Jesus said, "'Love the Lord your God with all your heart and with all your soul and with all your mind.' This is the first and greatest commandment. And the second is like it: 'Love your neighbor as yourself.' All the Law and the Prophets hang on these two commandments" (Matthew 22:37–40). Jesus put the first four commandments of the Decalogue into His first commandment, and the final six commandments of the Decalogue that have to do with our horizontal relationships in life — the royal law — into His second commandment. The royal law is not only given by the King of kings, but it is also the king of all laws. It is the law of love that governs those who are citizens of Christ's kingdom.

Since as Christians we are under this royal law of love, what exactly is our relationship to the law? The legalists say we are bound to it and, therefore, should meet on the Sabbath (which is Saturday). They say salvation is not obtained by grace through faith, but by following the law. On the opposite end of the spectrum are the libertarians, who say that they are totally free from the law. They cite Romans 6:14 as their flagship verse: "For sin shall not be your master, because you are not under law, but under grace." They lapse into what theologians call antinomianism ("against the law"). They think they are above the law.

Paul explained what the relationship of the Christian to the law should be: "What, then, was the purpose of the law? It was added because of transgressions until the Seed to whom the promise referred had come. The law was put into effect through angels by a mediator...Before this faith came, we were held prisoners by the law, locked up until faith should be revealed. So the law was put in charge to lead us to Christ that we might be justified by faith. Now that faith has come, we are no longer under the supervision of the law" (Galatians 3:19, 23–25).

The law was never given to save us. It was given to be our "schoolmaster" (KJV, παιδαγωγος). The NIV translates this Greek word as "put in charge." Παιδαγωγος could have been used in reference to a slave whose duty it was to see that a child made it to school safely and returned home at the end of the day. The law showed God's people how futile it was to think that they could get to Heaven by their own works — by keeping all the law. Thus, the law supervised their spiritual growth until the Messiah came. The law was the schoolmaster whose task was to bring people to Christ.

Does this mean that since Jesus has come we do not have to obey the law today? It means that Christians are under the royal law of love. Jesus did not do away with the law for Christians. In fact He said, "Do not think that I have come to abolish the Law or the Prophets; I have not come to abolish them but to fulfill them. I tell you the truth, until heaven and earth disappear, not the smallest letter, not the least stroke of a pen, will by any means disappear from the Law until everything is accomplished" (Matthew 5:17–18). Jesus made the law a matter of the heart. He made it a matter of love. This was the original intention of God — the lawgiver — in the first place.

Paul wrote: "It is for freedom that Christ has set us free. Stand firm, then, and do not let yourselves be burdened again by a yoke of slavery" (Galatians 5:1). The Christian is not governed by external laws and rules, but by the internal royal law — the law of love. When he loves God with all his heart and loves his neighbor as himself, he will certainly live within the parameters of the moral code of the Mosaic law.

According to the royal law, discrimination is sin. If a person discriminates against others, he does not have a leg on which to stand.

Presumption Number Two: Discrimination Is Not Significant

Often people who discriminate are so blinded by what they feel that they think their sin is not significant. They reason, "So what...it's not like I murdered somebody or committed adultery; it's insignificant." What a presumption! James said that discrimination is significant. In fact, he said that a person who discriminates is a lawbreaker like an adulterer or murderer.

James was writing to people who had the erroneous idea that petty sins of disrespect, favoritism and discrimination are not significant. But James made clear what God really thinks about all types of sin.

Some people in our day seek to classify sin into different categories. Up at the top is murder, followed by adultery and then perhaps by stealing, etc. Down on the bottom of the list is discrimination. But God is revealing to us that one sin, no matter how insignificant we may think it to be, is significant: "For whoever keeps the whole law and yet stumbles at just one point is guilty of breaking all of it. For he who said, 'Do not commit adultery,' also said, 'Do not murder.' If you do not commit adultery but do commit murder, you have become a lawbreaker" (James 2:10–11). Without the mercy of God and the grace of the Lord Jesus Christ, one sin — no matter how small — is enough to condemn a person eternally. Jesus died for the sin of discrimination as much as for any other sin.

Many self-righteous people presume that because they have lived lives free of what society considers significant sins (murder, rape and the like), God will just smile and pass over the sin of discrimination. If any of us share this presumption, we should look again at James 2:10.

James said if we "stumble" over just one law, it is as though we have broken all the laws. The Greek word translated "stumble," πταίω, means "to trip" and suggests a picture of a long road that is paved but has some rough spots over which the traveler stumbles.[5] It doesn't matter that most of the road is paved if there is still a little patch that causes him to trip along the way. Πταίω also occurs in 2 Peter 1:10: "Therefore, my brothers, be all the more eager to make your calling and election sure. For if you do these things, you will never *fall*" *(italics added)*. The point is, one little sin is like a rough place in the road. Even though all the rest of life's road is smooth, that one place can cause one to fall on his face.

D. L. Moody compared God's law to a 10-link chain onto which a man was holding while suspended over a great cliff. Moody said if all 10 links were to break, the man would fall to his death. But if only one link were to break, the man would fall just as far and just as fast.

James 2:10 should put to rest the idea that any of us can get to Heaven on the basis of good works, reputation or morality. We have all sinned and fall short of the glory of God (Romans 3:23) and thus we are all guilty of breaking all the law. We all need the redemptive work of Jesus. Perhaps Paul said it best: "All who rely on observing the law are under a curse, for it is written: 'Cursed is everyone who does not continue to do everything written in the Book of the Law.' Clearly no one is justified before God by the law, because, 'The righteous will live by faith.' The law is not based on faith; on the contrary, 'The man who does these things will live by them.' Christ redeemed us from the curse of the law by becoming a curse for us, for it is written, 'Cursed is everyone who is hung on a tree.' He redeemed us in order that the blessing given to Abraham might come to the Gentiles through Christ Jesus, so that by faith we might receive the promise of the Spirit" (Galatians 3:10–14).

It is strange how some people think that they can stand before the Judge of the universe and appeal to Him on the basis of the sins which they have not committed. That reasoning will go about as far with God as it would with a municipal judge if a person tried to get out of a speeding ticket by saying, "Judge, it is true that I broke the law and was going 60 miles per hour in a 20 mile-per-hour school zone. But look at it this way — I never robbed a bank."

To be a lawbreaker, one does not have to break all the laws — only one. But to be a law-abider, one must keep all the laws. One way to break the royal law of love is to discriminate. Discrimination is a sin and it is significant. We must not presume otherwise.

Presumption Number Three: Discrimination Is Not Serious

Some people are presumptuous enough to think that although discrimination may be sin and may be significant, it is really not serious. James challenged anyone who thinks this way to wake up. In God's eyes, discrimination is very serious.

James 2:12–13 says, "Speak and act as those who are going to be judged by the law that gives freedom, because judgment without mercy will be shown to anyone who has not been merciful. Mercy triumphs over judgment!" Which judgment was James referring to in these verses? After all, several judgments are mentioned in Scripture.

There is the judgment of the believer's sin (John 5:24). The Bible tells us that the believer will not come into condemnation because his sins have already been judged on Calvary's cross. There is also the judgment seat of Christ (2 Corinthians 5:9–10) when the believer's works will be judged. Then there is the judgment of the nations (Matthew 25:31–32). This is not the final judgment of the lost, but the judgment that will deal with how people have treated the elect of Israel — the ones whom Jesus calls "these brothers of mine" in Matthew 25:40. This judgment will determine who can enter into the kingdom age and will be based on the nations' treatment of Israel during the period of tribulation. Finally, there is the judgment of the great white throne (Revelation 20:11–15), when the lost will be judged.

James was referring to the judgment seat of Christ. There our words will be judged: "But I tell you that men will have to give account on the day of judgment for every careless word they have spoken. For by your words you will be acquitted, and by your words you will be condemned" (Matthew 12:36–37). Our works will also be judged at the judgment seat of Christ: "Each one should be careful how he builds...his work will be shown for what it is, because the Day will bring it to light. It will be revealed with fire, and the fire will test the quality of each man's work. If what he has built survives, he will receive his reward. If it is burned up, he will suffer loss; he himself will be saved, but only as one escaping through the flames" (1 Corinthians 3:10,13–15).

Because of the judgment to come, it is presumptuous to say that discrimination is not serious. James 2:12 is a call to action here. It says that we are to "*speak* and *act* as those who are going to be judged" *(italics added)*. These two verbs are in the continuous tense, which means that we are to keep on speaking and keep on acting. We should respond to the call with our lips — in our speech. We should respond with our lives — through our actions.

How can we speak and act as we should? By obeying the royal law, that "law that gives freedom" (James 2:12). We are to love God with all our hearts and our neighbors as ourselves. If we obey the law of love, we will want to obey all of God's other laws.

This royal law brings freedom. On the surface, law and liberty seem to stand in opposition to one another. They appear to be enemies. After all, law restrains liberty, and liberty seems to imply being freed from the law. But James was saying that law and liberty come together in beautiful harmony. The way to be really free is to live within the boundaries of God's law. When we do, we are free indeed. When we are really disciples of Jesus, we know the truth and the truth sets us free (John 8:31–32).

Those who live outside the parameters of God's law, on the other hand, are not really free. They cover over one lie with another lie. They are trapped into covering over one sin with another sin until they become slaves to a lifestyle of sinning. Yes, sin is serious and will be judged.

Yet James 2:13 says, "Mercy triumphs over judgment."

If we show mercy to others in our speech and actions, we will triumph at the end at the judgment seat of Christ. The Greek word translated "triumph," κατακαυχάομαι, literally means "to have no fear of."[6] Merciful people have no fear of judgment. The one who shows mercy in this life is not afraid of that day when he will stand before the great Judge who knows the secrets of all men's hearts. Yes, mercy triumphs over judgment.

But remember, James was talking here about the judgment of believers' works, not the judgment of sin. We are not saved by being merciful. We are saved by receiving mercy from Christ, and when we have received His mercy, we will show mercy.

If we are unmerciful — if we are guilty of discrimination — what can we do? Many say, "It's in my background." Well, just because your father was an adulterer, you do not have to be. Just because your father may have been a murderer, you do not have to be. We must deal with discrimination by seeing it as it is. It is sin. Thus, we must deal with it like any other sin. After we admit it, confess it and forsake it, we will begin to speak and act like followers of Christ. The church today needs to speak against discrimination and act against it by reaching out to others in mercy.

Thank God that Jesus was no respecter of persons. He did not show favoritism. He reached out to society's richest and poorest with the same intensity. I am so thankful He did not discriminate against me because of my race, my resources, my respectability or the religion of my birth. Paul said, "For you know the grace of our Lord Jesus Christ, that though he was rich, yet for your sakes he became poor, so that you through his poverty might become rich" (2 Corinthians 8:9). He showed mercy toward us with His lips and with His life. He spoke the world's greatest words and backed them up by going to the cross.

At Calvary the ground is level for the rich and poor alike. As Sunday school children sing, "Red and yellow, black and white, they are precious in His sight." Remember, in the end "mercy triumphs over judgment."

··
⊛ CHAPTER FIVE ⊛
··

THE ETHICAL EFFECT
JAMES 2:14–26

I. A Faith Without Fruit Is a False Faith (James 2:14–17)
II. A Faith Without Fruit Is a Futile Faith (James 2:18–19)
III. A Faith Without Fruit Is a Fatal Faith (James 2:20–26)

We live in a day when everyone seems to be involved in an "effect" of some kind. There is the "greenhouse effect" with its future repercussions on our climate and environment. We have heard a lot about the "domino effect" as country after country in Eastern Europe has stood up to the tyranny of communism. The church today is faced with what I call the "ethical effect": faith without fruit. So many people profess one thing but practice another. So many people fake their faith and forfeit their fruit.

In more and more cities, the church is losing its place of respect and influence. At one time the church was a leader in civic affairs. Now, because of the ethical effect, it has been relegated to the back row of the auditorium of influence. The church talks about faith but seldom produces its fruit. While many church members are quick to say they are people of faith, the world shouts back with the haunting question of James 2:16: "What good is it?"

Because the church has lost its voice in so many communities, our whole nation is involved in an ethical effect. An integrity crisis is running rampant and its tentacles have reached into every strata of society. The ethical effect has touched the world of sports, business, government, law, medicine, politics and unfortunately the world of religion. Volumes could be written to illustrate the ethical failures in the above fields. Our world is watching and waiting for a voice whose life matches its lips and whose walk matches its talk. This is the church's great opportunity.

Currently, the big controversy in ecclesiastical circles seems to be over the nature of salvation. People tend to gravitate toward one of two extreme views. One extreme overemphasizes faith while forgetting works; the other overemphasizes works while forgetting faith. The former is referred to as "easy believism." Proponents of this soteriology think that one can say a simple "sinner's prayer" and have no change of lifestyle, never pray again, never open a Bible, never have any desire for spiritual things and still be saved because he believed. The latter is referred to as "works salvation." Proponents of this soteriology think that one must earn his way into eternal life.

The conflict between faith and works is age-old. The whole argument originated in the issue addressed in James 2:14–26. The Bible plainly and repeatedly teaches that salvation is by grace through faith in the Lord Jesus Christ alone. However, the Bible also clearly teaches that true saving faith will always result in good works.

The faith-and-works dispute arises when people fail to make a distinction between the requirement for true salvation and the result of true salvation. Good works are not the requirement for true salvation, but they are certainly the result. It is impossible for someone to have a new birth experience, move from darkness into light and from death into life, see old things pass away, have all his sins forgiven, have the God of the universe take up residence within his life and still not alter his lifestyle or his inner desires one iota. The apostle John said that if we are truly saved, we will not continue in repetitive sin.

The ethical effect, faith without fruit, is the burden of James 2:14–26. Many people falsely think James was speaking about a faith *with* works. But he was speaking about a faith *that* works. If you remember that distinction, you will understand James' discussion of the ethical effect. The church today needs a faith that works — a faith with accompanying fruit.

James shows us that faith without fruit is false, futile and fatal.

I. A Faith Without Fruit Is a False Faith
James 2:14–17

 An Explanation

James began his discussion of the ethical effect by asking, "What good is it, my brothers, if a man claims to have faith but has no deeds? Can such faith save him?" (James 2:14). A faith without any fruit is false. Earlier the Lord Jesus said the same thing in a different way: "By their fruit you will recognize them. Do people pick grapes from thornbushes, or figs from thistles? Likewise every good tree bears good fruit, but a bad tree bears bad fruit. A good tree cannot bear bad fruit, and a bad tree cannot bear good fruit. Every tree that does not bear good fruit is cut down and thrown into the fire. Thus, by their fruit you will recognize them" (Matthew 7:16–20).

Carefully note what James was saying. He was not speaking about a man who has faith, but about a man who "claims" to have faith. James put the emphasis on a false claim to faith and not on the true nature of faith. He contrasted what a person claims to be and what he really is. The Greek verb tense indicates that the person keeps on making his claims, apparently for years. Merely claiming that we are Christians does not make us such. Many people claim to have faith but have never trusted Christ alone for their salvation. Jesus reminds us, "Not everyone who says to me, 'Lord, Lord,' will enter the kingdom of heaven, but only he who does the will of my Father who is in heaven" (Matthew 7:21).

Much of the confusion in the faith-and-works controversy results from the King James translation of the last phrase of James 2:14: "Can faith save him?" This translation appears to suggest that faith alone is insufficient to bring us to Christ, that it must be coupled with works. Many people use this translation of the verse as a proof text to show that faith is not enough. Then they add baptism, good works or any number of other things to the requirements for salvation.

But the NIV more accurately translates the question: "Can *such* faith save him?" *(italics added)*. In the Greek text there is an article in front of the word we translate "faith." The article indicates that this faith is the same as the faith just mentioned — a false faith. It is a faith that one only claimed to have. James was not saying that faith does not save. He was saying that a false faith (one with no fruit) cannot save.

The Greek word σώζω, translated "save" in James 2:14, means "to rescue or to save." In the aorist tense it means "to achieve salvation for him."[1] Sometimes σώζω refers to the judgment on the last day.[2] So James was saying that the faith some people claim to have will be of no profit on the judgment day. Jesus Himself said that He would say to many people on that day, "I never knew you" (Matthew 7:23).

Every Sunday people by the multiplied thousands say they have faith. But for many it is a faith without fruit. They carry their creeds around with them like identification badges and repeat them in lifeless churches. But James 2:14 asks, "What good is it, my brothers, if a man claims to have faith but has no deeds? Can such [false] faith save him?" The question can only be answered in the negative: "Of course not!" That particular kind of faith cannot save anyone. It is of no value because it is made up of all lips and no life, all talk and no walk. A faith with no works is a faith with no worth.

An Illustration

Having explained false faith, James proceeded to illustrate it. He told a hypothetical story about someone in need of the basic necessities of life — food and clothing. He is not a professional con artist with a slothful lifestyle; he has a legitimate need. A person who claims to have faith comes over, puts his hand on the fellow's shoulder, and says, "Have a good day; be careful; stay warm; I hope you find something to eat." Unfortunately, the person who claims to have faith does nothing about the needy person's physical needs.

What good is our faith if we never put it into action? The book of James calls us to examine ourselves to be sure our faith is not false. Let us not be among those who prefer words to works and fail the test of the ethical effect because their faith never produces fruit.

An Application

Saying "good luck" to a man who needs food doesn't relieve his hunger. "In the same way, faith by itself, if it is not accompanied by action, is dead" (James 2:17). That is, faith without fruit doesn't do you any good. You are saved by faith plus nothing, but a faith that produces no fruit is not a genuine faith. Likewise, your love for Christ is not genuine if you don't want to please Him. If you really love Him, you will want to express your love.

Jesus told the parable of the soils to illustrate the fallacy of a faith without fruit. He wanted to show us that in many cases those who claim to have faith only have a false faith. The story is about a sower who scattered seed. Some seeds fell on hardened ground; some seeds fell on rocky ground; some seeds fell on thorny ground; and some seeds fell on good ground. In each environment something happened to the seeds, but only the seeds that fell on good ground produced fruit. The other seeds ended up being worthless.

The only way to know if faith is genuine is by its fruit. We are not to judge whether someone else's faith is false or not. In fact, Jesus reminds us, "Do not judge, or you too will be judged" (Matthew 7:1). However, in the same chapter Jesus says, "By their fruit you will recognize them" (7:20). Although we are not to be judges, we certainly are to be fruit inspectors.

"Faith by itself" (James 2:17) is translated from the Greek ἑαυτοῦ. The phrase tells us that false faith is not outwardly operative because it is inwardly dead. Perhaps John Calvin said it best: "It is faith alone that justifies, but faith that justifies can never be alone." True saving faith will never be "by itself." It will produce fruit to accompany it.

Lawyers and judges would be quick to tell us that in a trial they cannot deal with hearsay. They look for evidence — hard, cold facts. I once heard this question: "If you were arrested for being a Christian, would there be enough evidence to convict you?" Think about it. Would there be anyone who could take the witness stand and say, "He came to my house when I was in need and shared the love of Christ," or "He got on his knees and led me to the Savior"? James said faith without fruit is a false faith.

One of the greatest evangelistic harvest fields in America just might be people on church rolls who claim to have faith but have not produced fruit. Remember, James was not talking about a faith with works, but a faith *that* works!

II. A Faith Without Fruit Is a Futile Faith
James 2:18–19

An Explanation

A faith without fruit is false, and it is also futile. According to James it is frustrating and futile simply to talk about faith. Using an imaginary person to take the other perspective, James continued to talk about someone who only says that he has faith (James 2:18). Again, it is all talk.

James answered the imaginary person's claim with this challenge: "Show me your faith without deeds, and I will show you my faith by what I do" (James 2:18). The word translated "by" is the Greek εκ, which means "emerging out of or emerging from."[3] James was saying that works emerge from true faith. Paul said the same: "For it is by grace you have been saved, through faith — and this not from yourselves, it is the gift of God — not by works, so that no one can boast. For we are God's workmanship, created in Christ Jesus to do good works, which God prepared in advance for us to do" (Ephesians 2:8–10). In verses 8–9, Paul said faith alone is necessary for salvation. However, in verse 10, he talked about fruit. Neither James nor Paul was talking about a faith with works, but a faith that works. A man is saved by grace through faith unto good works.

At first James 2:18 appears to contradict Paul's statement in Romans 3:28: "For we maintain that a man is justified by faith apart from observing the law." In reality, they are complementing, not contradicting each other. When we examine these statements in context, we find that James and Paul arrived at the same point from different perspectives.

They said the same things, but with different emphases. For example, when Paul spoke of works he was referring to the works of the law, such as observing the Sabbath and offering required sacrifices. However, when James spoke of works, he was referring to the fruit of our faith, which is obedience that issues out of love.

Paul was hitting hard at men and women who try to be saved by keeping the law instead of trusting Christ alone for salvation. James, on the other hand, was concerned with people who confuse mere intellectual assent with true saving faith that will ultimately produce fruit. If Paul were alive today, he would address his argument to those who are overbalanced on the side of "works salvation." If James were alive today, he would address his argument to those who are overbalanced on the side of the "easy believism" of the antinomians who say, "I'm saved and I can live any way I desire."

An Illustration

James illustrated a futile faith with demons, of all things. He said, "You believe that there is one God. Good! Even the demons believe that — and shudder" (James 2:19). It may surprise some of us to discover that demons have faith — that they believe there is one God. They are not atheists or agnostics. In fact, they believe in the deity of Christ as evidenced in Matthew 8:29: "'What do you want with us, Son of God?' they shouted." The possessed man in the synagogue in Capernaum said, "What do you want with us, Jesus of Nazareth? Have you come to destroy us? I know who you are — the Holy One of God!" (Mark 1:24). When Jesus was healing people near Galilee, it is recorded that "whenever the evil spirits saw him, they fell down before him and cried out 'You are the Son of God'" (Mark 3:11). Luke 4:41 says, "Moreover, demons came out of many people, shouting, 'You are the Son of God!'"

Yes, evil spirits believe. They recognize the holiness of God and the deity of Christ, but they do not have a saving faith. Their faith is merely intellectual assent that goes no further than head knowledge. Describing the demons' belief, James used the word πιστεύω , which means "to make a mere profession of faith without a change of heart or behavior."[4]

Demons not only believe; they also "shudder" (φρίσσω). James 2:19 is the only place this word is used in the New Testament. Φρίσσω means "to demonstrate a high degree of awe or terror."[5] It means "to bristle up" and was used by ancient Greek writers to describe hair that stands on end. The point is that even though demons have only intellectual assent and not true saving faith, at least they respond; they shudder in terror of the coming judgment.

Many professing believers today are farther from God than the demons. These people give intellectual assent to Christ's claims, but have never truly been born again. Almost robotically they recite their creeds, but they have no fear of God. Perhaps most of the people in Hell at one time claimed to believe in God. They were not atheists or agnostics while on earth. They were simply folks who had a false and futile faith.

An Application

It is possible (and more likely probable) that most of us gave mental, intellectual assent to the claims of the gospel before our conversion to Christ. We believed the facts about the Lord Jesus. We were not agnostics or atheists. But for many of us the gospel meant nothing. It did not alter our lives. We believed that Jesus died on the cross in the same way that we believed that George Washington was the first president of the United States.

Perhaps you have believed for years but have never been

truly born again. You have never passed from death unto life or from spiritual darkness into light. Your faith is futile and worthless. The tragedy is that, unlike the shuddering Satanic forces, your false belief may not really bother you. If this is the case, allow Christ to transform your life and produce fruit in and through you. Ask God to give you a faith that works.

III. A Faith Without Fruit Is a Fatal Faith
James 2:20–26

An Explanation

A faith without fruit is not simply false and futile; it is fatal. In the words of James 2:26, it is "dead." There are no vital signs — no pulse rate, no heartbeat. There is only fatal silence.

James 2:20 says that a man who has a faith without fruit is "foolish." The Greek word translated "foolish" is κενός, which means "empty or deficient." The word is used to describe an undependable imposter. Κενός occurs in Mark 12:3: "But they seized him, beat him and sent him away *empty-handed*" *(italics added)*. It is also used in Luke 1:53: "He has filled the hungry with good things but has sent the rich away *empty*" *(italics added)*. The point is, if a man only says he has faith, he is empty.

James 2:20 also says that such faith is "useless." The Greek word translated "useless" is ἀργός which literally means "not working or idle."[6] Such faith is dead — fatal.

An Illustration

Having challenged his readers to recognize a fatal faith, James provided two Old Testament illustrations to prove that real faith is accompanied by fruit. He reminded us of a faithful patriarch, Abraham, and a former prostitute, Rahab.

James 2:21 says, "Was not our ancestor Abraham considered righteous for what he did when he offered his son Isaac on the altar?" Again there appears to be a discrepancy between the theology of Paul and the theology of James. For example, Paul seemed to counter James in Romans 4:1–3: "What then shall we say that Abraham, our forefather, discovered in this matter? If, in fact, Abraham was justified by works, he had something to boast about — but not before God. What does the Scripture say? 'Abraham believed God, and it was credited to him as righteousness.'" These two statements are actually complementary.

James was not answering Paul here, as some theologians have accused. James wrote his letter as early as A.D. 48, and Paul did not write the Roman letter until at least A.D. 58. James and Paul were coming from two different perspectives. Paul was writing to Judaizers who were saying that one had to add works of the law to faith in order to receive salvation. Thus his emphasis was on faith alone. He was arguing for the primacy of faith. James, on the other hand, was writing to people who went to the other extreme. They claimed to have faith but had only intellectual assent. Therefore his emphasis was on what Jesus called the fruit of our faith. He was simply arguing for the proof of faith.

Paul emphasized that no one enters God's kingdom except by faith. James agreed and, as we saw earlier, said so: "He chose to give us birth through the word of truth, that we might be a kind of firstfruits of all he created" (James 1:18). In chapter 2, James just reinforced the point that good works are the natural response of those who are truly in God's family. In context, James was not saying that works are a requirement for salvation, but that they are the result of salvation. This is what Jesus said in Matthew 7:20: "Thus, by their fruit you will recognize them."

Paul, as we saw earlier, used the word "works" to mean a

legalistic observance of the Jewish law. James used the same word to mean the fruit of our salvation. When we look at the passages in context, we see that both men were simply looking at the same situation from two perspectives.

Now let's continue to look at the relationship between Abraham's faith and his actions. James 2:22 says, "You see that his faith and his actions were working together." The Greek word for "working together," συνεργέω, means "to cooperate, to work together." It is the same word Paul used in Romans 8:28: "And we know that in all things God works for the good of those who love him, who have been called according to his purpose." Abraham's faith was active and working.

James 2:22 adds, "And his faith was made complete by what he did." Does this mean that we are not complete in Christ by faith alone? The Greek word translated "made complete," τελειόω, means "to consummate, to complete, to bring to maturity."[7] It means "to carry to the end."[8] Thus faith ultimately ends up producing fruit. They work together to be made complete.

James 2:23 continues, "And the scripture was fulfilled that says, 'Abraham believed God, and it was credited to him as righteousness,' and he was called God's friend." James was quoting Genesis 15:6 to make his point. And Paul quoted the same verse to make his point: "What does the Scripture say? 'Abraham believed God, and it was credited to him as righteousness'" (Romans 4:3). Paul was saying that Abraham was justified by faith. James certainly did not disagree; he was simply adding that this faith was evidenced by fruit.

What happened in Genesis 15:6? It records the time of Abraham's salvation. At that time he believed God's promise. He was saved by faith in God's promise, as we are. The only difference is that Abraham was looking forward to Christ's promise of redemption on the cross, and we are looking backward to it.

Having believed the promise in Genesis 15, Abraham was put to the test by God some 30 years later. God called Abraham to take his son Isaac up Mount Moriah. Abraham obeyed God completely and Hebrews 11:17 records: "By faith Abraham, when God tested him, offered Isaac as a sacrifice. He who had received the promises was about to sacrifice his one and only son." It is this incident in Genesis 22 that James had in mind when he said, "Was not our ancestor Abraham considered righteous for what he did when he offered his son Isaac on the altar?" (James 2:21) James was not discussing how a person becomes a believer. He was discussing the way in which one produces what Paul later called the "fruit of righteousness" (Philippians 1:11). In Genesis 15, Abraham said, "I believe." In Genesis 22, he showed his belief.

Seeking to clarify Abraham's justification before God, Paul said, "If, in fact, Abraham was justified by works, he had something to boast about — but not before God" (Romans 4:2). On the other hand, James wanted to show how Abraham was justified as a witness in front of men, thus giving evidence of true faith. Consequently, James said, "You see that a person is justified by what he does and not by faith alone" (James 2:24). James' emphasis was on our showing the fruit of our faith. This is also Jesus' emphasis in Matthew 5:16: "Let your light shine before men, that they may see your good deeds and praise your Father in heaven." Visible fruit is simply the outward evidence of a vital faith. Salvation comes by faith in Christ alone, and true faith produces fruit.

Abraham was considered righteous, but he was not righteous in himself. Romans 3:10 reminds us, "There is no one righteous, not even one," but Abraham's faith was "credited" (λογίζομαι) to him as righteousness (James 2:23). The Greek word translated "credited" is an accountant's term, a financial expression that means "to put on one's account." Abraham's spiritual bank account was depleted. He was spiritually bankrupt. But he trusted in God, and God made a deposit in his account. God put His own righteousness into Abraham's account. Abraham didn't work for it. He received it as a gift. This is exactly what happens to us when we become Christians. All of our righteousness is imputed righteousness; it is given to us by God on the basis of our faith.

Let's say that someone overextends himself with a credit card and cannot pay the dollars due. When the bill comes, he dreads opening the envelope. However when he finally does, he discovers that someone else has already paid the bill in full and has deposited an amount that can be drawn from and charged against! This is a picture of how righteousness is credited to our accounts when we believe. Our accounts were full of debts we could not pay. We had charged to our accounts the sins of our lives. But Jesus went to Calvary and paid a debt He did not owe because we owed debts we could not pay.

Did Abraham believe that Jesus Christ was the Messiah? I'll say he did because Jesus said he did: "Your father Abraham rejoiced at the thought of seeing my day; he saw it and was glad" (John 8:56). Because Abraham had a genuine faith that resulted in good works, he was recognized as God's friend.

James 2:24 adds, "You see that a person is justified by what he does and not by faith alone." Here again is an apparent discrepancy between Paul and James. Paul appears to be in diametric opposition in his Roman writings. But James was again approaching the issue from a different angle. He was saying that mere verbal assent with no fruit is dead, barren and useless. This is what he meant by "faith alone." Paul and James were not conflicting with one another; they were complementing one another. Paul contended that we are made righteous without the help of works. And he was right! James contended that those who profess faith but have no fruit whatsoever, are not declared righteous simply because they give assent to the gospel; even the demons do that. And he was right! The word "alone" in James 2:24 does not mean works are a requirement for salvation, but that they are a result of salvation. Remember, Paul and James were coming from two different perspectives. Paul was writing to Judaizers who were saying that works of the law had to be added to faith; thus his emphasis was on faith alone. James was writing to people who went to the other extreme and claimed to have a faith when they only had an intellectual assent; thus his emphasis was on what Jesus called the "fruit of our faith."

James referred to Abraham to prove that real faith is accompanied by fruit. For the same reason, he told the story of Rahab. "In the same way, was not Rahab the prostitute considered righteous for what she did when she gave lodging to the spies and sent them off in a different direction?" (James 2:25) In contrast to Abraham, Rahab was known for her immorality instead of her morality. She was outside the Jewish covenant, not inside. She was rejected by society, not respected. She was a former prostitute, not a faithful patriarch. Yet James' words, "in the same way," show Abraham and Rahab's similarity in faith. Even though they came from different paths of life, they both came to Christ the same way — by faith. The richest of the rich and the poorest of the poor come through the same door. The most moral and the most immoral come through the same door of faith.

Rahab came to faith in the living God before she hid Joshua's messengers. Listen to her testimony: "Before the spies lay down for the night, she went up on the roof and said to them, 'I know that the Lord has given this land to you and that a great fear of you has fallen on us, so that all who live in this country are melting in fear because of you. We have heard how the Lord dried up the water of the Red Sea for you when you came out of

Egypt, and what you did to Sihon and Og, the two kings of the Amorites east of the Jordan, whom you completely destroyed. When we heard of it, our hearts melted and everyone's courage failed because of you, for the Lord your God is God in heaven above and on the earth below'" (Joshua 2:8–11).

On the basis of that faith, Rahab produced fruit. She received God's messengers and sent them on their way. She proved her faith by her fruit. She had good works, not simply good words. Hiding the messengers did not earn her salvation because she was already saved. If there is any question about this, Hebrews 11:31 settles it forever: "By faith the prostitute Rahab, because she welcomed the spies, was not killed with those who were disobedient." Her salvation was by faith...and fruit resulted.

When judgment came to Jericho, there was one part of the wall that judgment could not touch because the scarlet cord hung in Rahab's window. Rahab went on to live among the Israelites and she married Salmon. Their son Boaz had a son named Obed who had a son named Jesse who had a son named David, from whom the lineage of Jesus descended. What amazing grace! And it all began when Rahab heard the word of the Lord. She had just a tiny fragment, but she believed it and was saved.

Some who claim to have faith have no desire to serve God. But Rahab believed that God was going to give Israel the land, and her faith in Him caused her to react as she did. Her faith caused her to act. It was real. She was not saved by a faith with works, but by a faith *that* worked.

In these two illustrations, both the faithful patriarch and the former prostitute were declared righteous on the basis of their faith, which was proved by the fruit they produced. They were justified by a faith that worked.

True faith always produces fruit. Abraham believed and, therefore, he was willing to sacrifice Isaac. Rahab believed and, therefore, she hid the messengers. In the faith chapter of Hebrews 11, each verse begins with "By faith" and concludes with an act of obedience. Everyone mentioned in the chapter responded by faith and immediately demonstrated obedience. Faith is not real until it moves us into action. Faith without fruit is simply false, futile and fatal.

An Application

James concluded his discourse on faith and works with these words: "As the body without the spirit is dead, so faith without deeds is dead" (James 2:26). James tied a bow on the ethical effect — a faith without fruit — by saying that faith and fruit are as essential to each other as the body and the spirit. God never created a body without a soul, and a mere profession of faith without fruit is evidence that such faith is fatal. It is nothing more than a corpse.

In the ancient world, someone finding a person who appeared to be dead would hold a mirror under the person's nose. If marks appeared on the mirror, he knew the body was still alive though barely breathing. If no marks appeared, he knew the body was dead and good for nothing. Left unburied, the body would sour, stink and spread disease. James took the mirror of God's Word and put it under the nose of one who claimed to have faith to see if anything appeared. If nothing appeared — if no fruit was produced — that faith was dead; it was good for nothing. If others could see the faith breathing...moving...acting, that faith was alive.

The preservation of dead bodies is called mortuary science. Experts who are skilled at beautifying and preserving dead bodies try to make them look lifelike — alive. How many times have we heard these words at a funeral: "Oh, doesn't she look natural?" Or, "He looks as if he could speak." Likewise, many men and women whose faith is really dead try to look as much as possible like people who are alive. They recite creeds accurately, and they teach them to their children. They pretend to be alive spiritually by referring to some "decision" they made years ago. Yet they live their lifetimes without trusting Christ and with false hope. They are like dead bodies trying to look like something they aren't. Like dead bodies, they don't do anybody any good, and they quickly become offensive.

Many church members today have no faith and no works. Some gather to say their creeds and talk about faith and positive thinking, but they have no ongoing ministries to meet people's needs. Others have works without faith. Their approach is motivated simply by social or humanistic values. Biblical Christianity, as we have seen, is not a faith with works; it is a faith that works.

In his devotional commentary on the book of James, *How to Solve Conflicts,* George Sweeting told the story of Blondin, the great tightrope walker. While performing on a cable across Niagara Falls, he asked his audience, "How many of you believe I can walk across the cable pushing a wheelbarrow?" The people cheered and raised their voices. "How many believe I can push the wheelbarrow across the cable with a man in the wheelbarrow?" Again the audience cheered and raised their hands. Blondin then pointed to one enthusiastic gentleman and said, "You're my man. Get into the wheelbarrow." Needless to say, the man made a rapid exit.[9] Millions of people are quick to claim a faith in Christ, but many are living with the ethical effect of a faith without fruit. So Jesus is saying, "Get into the wheelbarrow!"

In 1887 a young lad who was converted to Christ at a D. L. Moody meeting in Massachusetts stood up to give a testimony and said, "I intend to trust the Lord from this day forth and to obey Him and His word." When John H. Sammis heard of that testimony, he penned words that we have sung for over a century.

This chapter could be summed up in the lyrics of his hymn:

When we walk with the Lord in the light of His Word,
What a glory He sheds on our way!
While we do His good will, He abides with us still,
And with all who will trust and obey.

Trust and obey, for there's no other way
To be happy in Jesus,
But to trust and obey.

······································

⊛ **CHAPTER SIX** ⊛

······································

WORDS AS WELL AS WORKS
JAMES 3:1–12

I. Controlled Speech Is Directive (James 3:1–5)
II. Contentious Speech Is Destructive (James 3:5–8)
III. Conflicting Speech Is Deceptive (James 3:9–12)

There is a new phenomenon capturing the American public today. Radio and television talk shows dominate the media. We are a nation of talkers. People everywhere have something to say and want to be heard. In his second inaugural address, Richard Nixon said, "America has suffered from a fever of words. We cannot learn from one another until we stop shouting at one another, until we speak quietly enough that our words can be heard as well as our voices."[1] Long before President Nixon voiced those words, James put it like this: "My dear brothers, take note of this: Everyone should be quick to listen, slow to speak and slow to become angry" (James 1:19).

What comes out of our mouths is so vitally important that James devoted 12 entire verses to it in the middle of his letter. Having just dealt with the relationship of faith and works, James moved on to deal with the relationship of faith and words. Our words reveal what is actually in our hearts. James wanted us to know that it is not enough to have words without works and it is not enough to have works without words.

I went through elementary school, junior high school and high school with a boy who was what one might call the class wimp. Because he never engaged in any of the more manly athletic endeavors, he bore the brunt of a lot of ridicule and taunting. He would always respond to his harassers with the phrase, "Sticks and stones may break my bones, but words will never hurt me."

Many years later, after I came to know Christ, I learned that his statement was not true. I have several scars from wounds inflicted by sticks and stones. Those wounds all healed. Even the cut I received when another boy bounced a rock off my head healed, and I haven't thought about it in years. I have a scar on my leg from the time I fell over a picket fence and cut my leg wide open. On my left shin I have a large scar that is the result of someone sliding into second base with his spikes in the air. All those wounds have healed. But the class wimp and I have wounds from words that have never healed.

Words are powerful. How many children have heard their parents say, "You are worthless and will never amount to anything"? And the children believed their parents and allowed those words to shape their lives. How many other children have heard their parents say, "You are somebody. You are important as a person. You have important things to do in life"? And the children believed their parents. What we say has tremendous power — for good or bad.

James 3:1 confronts believers who substitute words for works: "Not many of you should presume to be teachers, my brothers, because you know that we who teach will be judged more strictly." Teachers will be judged more strictly if their works do not match their words. James warned teachers to make sure that they teach the truth and practice what they preach. Because teachers have received more spiritual light, they ought to live on a higher level of obedience to God and His laws.

Jesus considers careless speech to be a very serious matter (Matthew 12:36–37). Thus James made three statements about the tongue in James 3:1–12, and he gave two illustrations for each statement. (It is as if James were in a Jewish court, which requires two witnesses to substantiate a point.) The first statement is that controlled speech is directive, like a bit on a bridle and a rudder on a boat. Secondly, James wrote that contentious speech is destructive, like fire and poison. Thirdly, James wrote that conflicting speech is deceptive; he illustrated this statement with a spring of water and a fig tree.

I. Controlled Speech Is Directive
James 3:1–5

An Explanation

Controlled speech, like a bridle on a horse or a rudder on a ship, is directive. It sets us on course and gives us direction in life. A horse left to itself will never accomplish anything for anyone. But a bridled horse under its master's control can be useful for all sorts of purposes.

An Illustration

James 3:3 illustrates the directive nature of the tongue: "When we put bits into the mouths of horses to make them obey us, we can turn the whole animal." I understand this point well because as a boy I spent a great deal of time around horses on my uncle's ranch in Texas. I watched the cowhands "break" many horses. As most of us know, the bridle has a bit — a metal bar that goes into the horse's mouth. When the rider wants the horse to halt, he pulls back on the reins and the bit presses against the horse's tongue. So the rider who controls the horse's tongue controls his whole body and can steer him to the right or left or bring him to a stop.

A horse controlled by a bit can be of great use. However, an uncontrolled horse can do great damage. Psalm 39:1 says, "I will watch my ways and keep my tongue from sin; I will put a muzzle on my mouth as long as the wicked are in my presence."

The Greek word for "bridle" or "bit" means "to lead." We picture an animal unwilling to carry a load to its destination without leadership.[2] Sometimes our loads seem heavy. We, like horses, sometimes need the Master to lead us and give us direction.

No horse has ever bridled himself. Its master must do that. Likewise, try as we may, we cannot bridle ourselves. We need to yield our speech to the Master's control in order to receive direction in life. The bridle under a master's control benefits the horse by making him productive and leading him down the right path. Similarly, allowing the Master to control our tongues is for our own good.

James substantiated his teaching that controlled speech is directive with another illustration. "Or take ships as an example," he said. "Although they are so large and are driven by strong winds, they are steered by a very small rudder wherever the pilot wants to go" (James 3:4). The tongue is like the small rudder that guides a large ship. Isn't it amazing that something several inches long can make or break someone six feet tall?

Fort Lauderdale is home to one of the deepest water ports on the East Coast. At Port Everglades, there are always large naval vessels and supertankers from around the world. I was once a guest aboard a United States Navy destroyer that protects us from enemy submarines. It was 563 feet long, complete with helicopter pad, torpedoes and missile launchers. This mighty vessel of human ingenuity and engineering was guided in safe directions by a small rudder below the hull.

Thinking of sailboats, James reminded us that winds, not the rudder, propel the ship. Winds are necessary. A sailboat cannot get anywhere without them. In fact, the stronger the winds, the faster a boat can sail. However, a boat with no rudder is left to the mercy of the winds, has no direction and, thus, will never reach its destination. The implication is that strong winds are capable of causing a sailboat to crash on rocks hidden below the surface. None of us is immune to the strong winds of the storms of life. We, too, need a rudder.

The tragedy is that some of us have no real pilot at the control of our lives to steer us in the right direction when strong winds howl against us. Many of us have spent our entire lives at the wheel, trying to make all the decisions and call all the shots. How we need to make the words of Edward Hopper's song our prayer:

> *Jesus, Savior, pilot me*
> *Over life's tempestuous sea;*
> *Unknown waves before me roll,*
> *Hiding rock and treach'rous shoal;*
> *Chart and compass come from Thee;*
> *Jesus, Savior, pilot me.*

The winds blow to benefit us. When our Captain is at the wheel, winds drive us faster toward the goal. However, if God is not at the wheel, the same winds can cause us to get off course, capsize and sink.

An Application

James 3:5 says, "Likewise the tongue is a *small part* of the body, but it makes great boasts" *(italics added)*. The Greek word translated "small part," μελος, also means "melody, the music to which a song is set." God created the tongue to produce melody. If the tongue is out of tune, life has no melody. If we say one thing and do another, there is no music. Words and works should blend together.

The tongue is so small, and yet it has so much potential. No wonder Solomon said, "The tongue has the power of life and death" (Proverbs 18:21). Recognizing the importance of godly speech, David said, "Set a guard over my mouth, O Lord; keep watch over the door of my lips" (Psalm 141:3). When we yield to the control of our Master, He keeps us on course.

How we all need to come under the control of the Master! Just as the bit and the rudder are each under the control of a master, we should allow the Lord Jesus Christ to control our hearts (the wheels) so that our tongues (the rudders) move in His direction. How important it is that we use our tongues to direct people to the Lord Jesus Christ.

While a massive oil tanker is still out in the Atlantic but nearing a port, a small bar pilot's boat leaves the port to meet the tanker. Upon arriving at the larger vessel, the bar pilot disembarks from his boat and climbs up on the tanker. There the captain who has piloted the great supertanker across the Atlantic steps aside. He allows the bar pilot to take over control of the wheel because he knows how to direct the ship into the harbor. The bar pilot knows where the deep water channels are. He knows where the ship is to be docked. Jesus is our bar pilot, yet too many of us are trying to steer our own ships into the harbor. Like the captain of the tanker, we need to step aside and turn over the control of our lives to our bar pilot.

II. Contentious Speech Is Destructive
James 3:5–8

An Explanation

Having spoken about the potential of the tongue for good, James warned that the tongue also has potential for evil.

Controlled speech is directive, but contentious speech is destructive. The illustrations of fire and poison support his case.

An Illustration

"Consider what a great forest is set on fire by a small spark. The tongue also is a fire, a world of evil among the parts of the body. It corrupts the whole person, sets the whole course of his life on fire, and is itself set on fire by hell" (James 3:5-6). One spark from a match or a cigarette tossed from a car window can ignite a raging forest fire. Spreading faster and farther than we could ever imagine, it destroys millions of dollars worth of timber and leaves a bare, black and scorched landscape in its path.

The tongue, James said, is like a fire. How many people have had reputations ruined by a word carelessly spoken? The impact of a word spreads fast and far. A word spoken in Dallas today could be repeated in Los Angeles tomorrow. Rumors fly faster and farther than we can imagine. The tongue, just like fire, gets out of control and does irreversible damage. Contentious speech is destructive. A tiny little word of rumor starts small but grows in influence. One lie has to cover another lie. Like a fire, improper words burn, hurt and destroy reputations and relationships.

James 3:7–8 says, "All kinds of animals, birds, reptiles and creatures of the sea are being tamed and have been tamed by man, but no man can tame the tongue." While on a preaching tour of Kenya in East Africa, I visited the Tsavo Game Park with a missionary friend. Driving through the bush, we saw lions in their natural habitat. It is amazing to think that we can capture these great kings of beasts and train them to jump through rings of fire and sit on command. Seeing elephants in their natural habitat makes it even more difficult for me to believe that we can train them to grab each other's tails and walk around in a circle, or stand on their hind legs on small boxes. Yes, we can train just about anything there is — except the tongue.

No man can tame the tongue, but Jesus can! It is natural for people to tame animals, but it takes a supernatural act of God to tame our tongues. Although we cannot do it on our own, the Lord Jesus can do it when we yield to Him. He can take a tongue of gossip and turn it into a tongue of glory. He can take a tongue of bitterness and make it a tongue of blessing.

James further substantiated his view that contentious speech is destructive by saying that the tongue is "full of deadly poison" (James 3:8). Certain kinds of poison work slowly and secretly until they kill.[3] The tongue is like that. When a few poisonous words are injected into a conversation, they slowly and secretly create havoc and destruction. Like a serpent's poison, the venom of an untamed tongue can kill reputations that have been years in the making. A few words spoken in antagonism can destroy relationships that have been built up over a lifetime. Yes, contentious speech is destructive.

An Application

James 3:6 reminds us that the fire of the tongue originates in Hell. This verse is the only place in the Bible outside the Gospels that the Greek word, γέεννα, is found. Gehenna is the name of the valley (outside the city walls southwest of Jerusalem) where pagans believed the false god, Moloch, lived. They would sacrifice to Moloch by throwing little children into his fiery arms. This valley was a place of refuse — the city dump — and was always smoldering with fire. Gehenna is a picture of Hell.

James is saying that the fire you start with your tongue — the gossip or slander — comes right out of Hell. Behind every spoken word of divisiveness, or filth, or rumor or even uncontrolled anger, is Satan himself, who is going about the business of destroying hearts, homes and hopes.

Uncontrolled fire destroys, but fire is not bad in itself. When controlled, it is beneficial. We heat our homes with it. We sterilize our instruments with it. We cook with it. Likewise, words can be used to bless or blast...to direct or destruct. Words can also be used to deceive.

III. Conflicting Speech Is Deceptive
James 3:9–12

An Explanation

The American Indians used the term "a forked tongue," to describe conflicting, deceptive speech. James 3:9–12 addresses the same issue. James described a man who praises the Lord for all that He has done for him, and in the next breath curses his neighbor. James said that in doing this, the man is deceiving himself. Conflicting speech is deceptive, and according to James 3:10, "This should not be!"

An Illustration

James 3:11 asks, "Can both fresh water and salt water flow from the same spring?" It is impossible for sweet and bitter water to come from the same opening. Much of our world lives in villages that have no running water. So it is a great blessing to have access to a spring that bubbles continually with fresh water. And it would be a terrible disappointment if the sweet water were to become bitter. A spring with both sweet and bitter water would be as deceptive as the mouth out of which come both praise and cursing.

James 3:12 asks another rhetorical question: "Can a fig tree bear olives, or a grapevine bear figs?" The answer is obviously, "No." Such inconsistency is impossible in the natural world, which operates according to basic laws of consistency and order. Just as the fruit of the tree shows what kind of root system it has, so our mouths show what is in our hearts. If there is deception in our hearts, our speech will be deceitful.

Conflicting speech may deceive for a while, but in the end we are going to reap what we sow. Jesus said, "No one can serve two masters. Either he will hate the one and love the other, or he will be devoted to the one and despise the other" (Matthew 6:24).

An Application

Like a spring or a tree, our tongues will produce words according to our inner nature. It is as impossible for salt water and sweet water to come out of the same spring or for olives to grow on a fig branch as it is for our tongues to produce what is not inside our hearts. If we bless and curse at the same time, something is desperately wrong. Evil speech can only emanate from an evil heart. A heart for God will not produce a tongue that lies, slanders, gossips and curses. Matthew 12:34 says, "Out of the overflow of the heart the mouth speaks." Our tongues should not be organs of inconsistency.

We deceive ourselves if we believe that we can get through life with forked tongues. Our tongues are good barometers of what is really in our hearts. Some of us think that because we made a decision for Christ years ago, everything is all right. Yet we all too often speak conflicting words.

If your speech is conflicting, then something is radically wrong with your heart. But you will not find a solution by simply trying to work on your vocabulary. Your speech is a symptom and not the source of the problem. Jesus says, "The things that come out of the mouth come from the heart, and these make a man 'unclean'" (Matthew 15:18). And Solomon said our hearts are "the wellspring of life" (Proverbs 4:23).

Only incompetent physicians treat symptoms and not sources of diseases. Medical doctors look at our tongues during physical examinations since if there is a problem anywhere in the body, it is often detected in the "film" on the tongue. However, a competent doctor does not just clean our tongues and send us on our way. He sets out to find the source of our problems and doesn't simply deal with the symptom.

If you have the symptom of conflicting speech, the source of the problem must be brought to the cross of Calvary. The cross can sweeten your heart and produce a life of works and words that are pleasing to God and a blessing to others. Oh that the words of Psalm 19:14 might be our continual prayer: "May the words of my mouth and the meditation of my heart be pleasing in your sight, O Lord, my Rock and my Redeemer."

Do you remember how the Israelites felt, having reached the oasis of Marah after three days in the desert? Thirsty and tired, they drank of the water, but it was bitter. Moses cried out to the Lord and He showed him a piece of wood. Moses cast the wood into the water, and God made the waters sweet (Exodus 15:22–27). That piece of wood is symbolic of the tree on which our Savior died. When cast into the bitter waters where we have lost so much as a result of our sin, the cross can still make the bitter waters in our lives sweet.

Remember, no matter how hard man tries, he cannot tame the tongue. Education can't do it. Turning over a new leaf can't do it. Nothing in the natural realm can do it. Only a supernatural transformation can do it. The Christian life is not a changed life; it is an exchanged life. God wants to remove our contentious, deceptive hearts and give us brand new hearts.

In this age of human achievement, our ingenuity has reached heights never dreamed of even a few years ago. We have split the atom and done incredible things with computers. We have been to the moon and back. We have developed spy satellites that can read a newspaper in someone's hand on Fifth Avenue in New York City. We have conquered the land. We have conquered the city. We are conquering space. Yet we have never been able to tame ourselves. Only Christ can enable us to control ourselves and cause our words to be constructive, honest and loving.

Because we are made with a void inside that only Jesus Christ can fill, the best thing we can do with our tongues is to confess Jesus Christ as Savior and Lord. Romans 10:9–10 says: "If you confess with your mouth, 'Jesus is Lord,' and believe in your heart that God raised him from the dead, you will be saved. For it is with your heart that you believe and are justified, and it is with your mouth that you confess and are saved." One day "every tongue [will] confess that Jesus Christ is Lord, to the glory of God the Father" (Philippians 2:11). Have you made that great confession? When Charles Wesley was converted, he was so thrilled that he penned these cherished words:

> *O for a thousand tongues to sing*
> *My great Redeemer's praise,*
> *The glories of my God and King,*
> *The triumphs of His grace!*

⊛ CHAPTER SEVEN ⊛

WISDOM
JAMES 3:13-18

I. The Wisdom of the World (James 3:13-16)
II. The Wisdom of the Word (James 3:17-18)

Today knowledge is exploding. More young people are graduating from college than in any previous generation. Textbooks and even the instant internet access to information are behind the times almost as soon as they are printed. We can travel farther and higher and faster than anyone before us. The computer age continues to advance at such a pace that technology is outdated with each passing month.

But in the midst of this explosion of knowledge, wisdom is practically nonexistent. Many people's lives are in shambles. Position, power and prosperity have not brought peace and purpose. Suicides and divorce rates are astronomical. In our modern world, where so many homes are disintegrating, so many hopes are smashed and so many dreams are dashed, we need wisdom above all else.

There is a difference between knowledge and wisdom. Knowledge is the accumulation of facts. Wisdom is the ability to take facts and put them into action at the point of need. There are two kinds of wisdom: a wisdom that emanates from the world's systems and philosophies and a wisdom that issues from the Word of God.

The world's wisdom is rooted in the secular, sensual and Satanic. In the words of James 3:15, "Such 'wisdom' does not come down from heaven but is earthly, unspiritual, of the devil." Worldly wisdom has helped to create the drug epidemic, the abortion holocaust, the national debt and many other plaguing problems.

Never have people needed wisdom more than today. But the wisdom we need today is the wisdom of the Word, not the wisdom of the world. Wisdom of the Word emanates from Heaven, not from the earth. The world's wisdom is natural, but the wisdom of the Word is supernatural. "The wisdom that comes from heaven," said James, "is first of all pure; then peace-loving, considerate, submissive, full of mercy and good fruit, impartial and sincere" (James 3:17). Such wisdom is the God-given ability to perceive the true nature of circumstances in order to apply the will of God to the issue at hand.

We all need this wisdom of the Word. Providers need God's wisdom to know how to gain financial stability. Partners need this wisdom to know how to be the kind of spouses God would have them to be. Parents need this wisdom of the Word to know how to lead their families in the way of righteousness. We all need this wisdom in order to make godly decisions every day.

The greatest need of young people today is wisdom. Most of life's major decisions — whom to marry, what vocation to pursue, for example — are not made during middle age after years of experience, but for many in the late teens or early twenties.

Knowing Jesus Christ gives the Christian a great advantage over the non-believer. The only wisdom a non-believer can use is the wisdom of the world, but a Christian has at his disposal the wisdom of the Word. What a tragedy that so many Christians make decisions using the wisdom of the world and neglect the overriding wisdom of the Word of God that is essential to their success.

How can we obtain this wisdom of the Word? Like Solomon, reportedly the wisest man who ever lived, we must ask for it. When young King Solomon went to Gibeon to build an altar and worship God, God said to him, "Ask for whatever you want me to give you" (1 Kings 3:5). Solomon could have asked for anything, but he answered, "Give your servant a discerning heart to govern your people and to distinguish between right and wrong" (3:9). Solomon asked for wisdom. He recognized it to be his greatest need. Years later he said, "Wisdom is supreme; therefore get wisdom" (Proverbs 4:7).

Once we have obtained this wisdom of the Word, we should "show it" (James 3:13). The word "show" means "to put on display, to exhibit." Our lives should exhibit purity, peace, patience, productivity and prudence. We should display virtues that are in sharp contrast to the prejudice, partisanship, pandemonium and perversion that are products of the wisdom of the world. Let's examine both kinds of wisdom and learn how to apply the wisdom of the Word to our everyday lives.

I. The Wisdom of the World
James 3:13–16

Its Origin

James 3:15 informs us that the wisdom of the world "does not come down from heaven but is earthly, unspiritual, of the devil." Do you see it? The wisdom of the world does not come from God. According to James 3:15, it has a threefold origin: it is earthly (secular), unspiritual (sensual) and of the devil (Satanic). We read about this same trio in Ephesians 2:1–3: the world, the flesh and the devil. First John 2:16 also refers to these three forces as "the cravings of sinful man [the lust of the flesh], the lust of his eyes and the boasting of what he has and does [the pride of life]." Perhaps these three motivating factors are best expressed by three words: money, sex and power. Some who would never be motivated by money or sex, crave power. Note

where James said this craving originates. It is "not from above."
The wisdom of the world originates in the secular, in the sensual
and in the Satanic.

In the Secular

The wisdom of the world is "earthly" (James 3:15). The
Greek word translated "earthly," ἐπίγειος, appears only seven
times in the New Testament. Speaking of the enemies of the
cross, Paul used the same word in Philippians 3:19: "Their
destiny is destruction, their god is their stomach, and their glory
is in their shame. Their mind is on *earthly things" (italics added).*

Wisdom that originates in the secular results in confusion.
Genesis 11:1–9 provides an example. In the hopes of making a
name for themselves, the ancients applied humanistic methods
and secular wisdom to get God's attention. Building a tower
seemed like the wise thing to do. But the tower of Babel was not
God's idea and, therefore, it brought about confusion and disorder.

Many years later, secular wisdom reasoned that it would be
wise to put King Saul's armor on young David when he was
about to fight Goliath (1 Samuel 17:38). However, it was not
God's wisdom and, therefore, it created confusion. Saul looked to
the wisdom of the world while David looked to the wisdom of the
Word. So often we seek to make our decisions in the same way as
Saul. Our earthly, worldly wisdom has its roots in the secular
world's systems of thought.

In the Sensual

The wisdom of the world is unspiritual (James 3:15). The
Greek word translated "unspiritual," ψυχικός, is an adjective
derived from psyche which means "the soul." We, of course, get

our word "psychology" from this word. In English we use two terms to differentiate between man's immaterial parts. One is "psyche," or "soul"; the other is "pneuma," or "spirit." James 3:15 refers to the psyche — that which animates the body, that which gives life. Animals have psyche, but not pneuma.

The ancients believed that man can be divided into three parts: spirit, soul and body. There is the σoμα (the body) comprised of physical flesh and bones. There is also the ψυχή (the soul) that animates the body, giving it life and personality. Finally, there is the πνεῦμα (the spirit) that only a human being possesses. The spirit is what differentiates man from animals. Man's spirit enables him to connect with God.

We often use the word "soul" in the same sense as the ancients used the word "spirit." But in the first-century Greek world, psyche meant sensual physical life — that which sees, hears, smells, touches and tastes. By referring to the ψυχή instead of the πνεῦμα, James was saying that the wisdom of the world is the same kind of wisdom that animals use. It is nothing more than natural instinct. There is no other thought than that of personal survival. Decisions are based merely on the senses — the sensual.

The thought occurs to me that I have never seen a mental hospital for animals. I have seen many animal hospitals, but never an animal psychiatric unit. Why? Could it be that the root cause of much mental illness is not man's psyche, but his πνεῦμα — the neglected spirit that only God can make right? The wisdom of the world, which originates in the secular and the sensual, ignores the spirit.

Worldly wisdom is perceived by our senses. It says, "If it feels good, do it." It places feelings above faith. It is sensual and unspiritual. Its philosophy is, I'll believe it when I can see it or touch it or smell it or taste it or hear it. It operates in the realm of the soul instead of the realm of the spirit. This type of wisdom does not connect man with God, the source of true wisdom. This connection is only made when man's spirit bears witness with His Spirit.

In the Satanic

The wisdom of the world is "of the devil" (James 3:15). The original word δαιμονιώδης literally means "pertaining to demons." This wisdom is demonic in origin.[1] Plainly put, the wisdom of the world finds its origin in the devil and not in God. Satan, the ruler of this world, is the power behind the wisdom of the world.

This wisdom began way back in the Garden of Eden when Satan successfully deceived Eve into using the wisdom of the world instead of the wisdom of the Word. The wisdom of the Word that she had received from God said, "You are free to eat from any tree in the garden; but you must not eat from the tree of the knowledge of good and evil, for when you eat of it you will surely die" (Genesis 2:16–17). The wisdom of the world, which was secular, sensual and Satanic, said, "You will not surely die" (3:4). Eve made her choice: "When the woman saw that the fruit of the tree was good for food and pleasing to the eye, and also desirable for gaining wisdom, she took some and ate it. She also gave some to her husband, who was with her, and he ate it" (3:6). Eve chose the wisdom of the world, and the result was the same as James 3:16 describes: "Envy and selfish ambition...disorder and every evil practice."

How did it happen? Satan's deceit created a selfish desire. A selfish desire resulted in a sinful decision. A sinful decision brought a sure defeat. Eve's choice had its roots in that which was secular, sensual and Satanic — the wisdom of the world.

Why do you think the theory of evolution is so popular among secularists today? Evolution is certainly not popular because it is supported by scientific data. There is little, if any, real substantive supporting evidence. The theory is popular because its origin is Satanic. It is the devil's attempt to explain everything that exists without crediting God. Those of us who have seen the miracle of childbirth and have contemplated on how two tiny specks of protoplasm can come together to form all the intricacies of a nervous system and circulatory system and the like, know that the creation of human life is a supernatural act of God and not a mere chance of science. But the wisdom of the world tells us that human life is the result of the natural process of evolution.

To believe in the Bible and evolution at the same time is virtually impossible. Why? Because their basic premises are in diametric opposition to each other. According to evolutionary theory (the wisdom of the world), man started out insignificant and is progressing upward. The Bible (the wisdom of the Word) says that man started out in paradise and in communion with God. Then sin came, causing him to fall and progress downward. The wisdom of the world and the wisdom of the Word are diametrically opposed.

The epitome of the wisdom of the world, the New Age movement, is nothing new. The movement's secular, sensual and Satanic roots are in ancient Babylon (modern-day Iraq). Its goal is self-beautification. It encourages people to search for wisdom in sinful things such as horoscopes. Moses warned: "Let no one be found among you who sacrifices his son or daughter in the fire, who practices divination or sorcery, interprets omens, engages in witchcraft, or casts spells, or who is a medium or spiritualist or who consults the dead. Anyone who does these things is detestable to the Lord, and because of these detestable practices the Lord your God will drive out those nations before you. You must be blameless before the Lord your God" (Deuteronomy 18:10–13).

Its Outcome

The wisdom of the world results in "envy," ζῆλος (James 3:16). The verb from which the noun ζῆλος is derived means "to boil or to bubble up." We get our word "zeal" from ζῆλος. Zeal has to do with fire. Fire can be good or bad. If a fire is under control, it can bring warmth on a cold night or cook a good meal. If a fire is out of control, it can destroy a house and bring it to ashes. And so it is with zeal. It can be constructive or destructive. Our zeal, our fire for God, can warm others. Worldly zeal (envy) can burn others.

Simply defined, envy is the displeasure we take in others' good fortune. For example, even though a man may not want a particular honor for himself, he does not want a certain person to receive it. This envy is rooted in the wisdom of the world. Envy motivated Cain to kill Abel. God had accepted Abel's sacrifice and not Cain's. Envy motivated Joseph's brothers to throw him into the pit and sell him to the Ishmaelites. Joseph was their father's favorite son.

Envy can be further illustrated by a game my friends and I played in my old boyhood neighborhood in Fort Worth, Texas. We called our game "King of the Hill." On the vacant lot on the corner of Crenshaw and Collard, there was a dirt mound about five feet high. One of us would stand on the mound and the rest of us would try to knock him off. I remember one particular boy who never really wanted to be on top of the hill, but who always delighted in knocking everybody else off. In the same way, the wisdom of the world manifests itself in envy. The object is to knock the other guy off the hill — even if we don't want to be on top.

Another result of applying the wisdom of the world to our lives is "selfish ambition," ἐριθεία (James 3:16). Εριθεία literally means a "party spirit" — pushing oneself forward for personal gain or glory.[2] The Greeks used this word to describe a politician who was canvassing for votes.[3] Derived from a verb used to describe those who politic for office,[4] ἐριθεία suggests a picture of one who achieves popular applause through trickery or plotting. In order to get their way, some people will say anything, anywhere, anytime. The English commentator William Barclay noted that in the first centuries ἐριθεία meant "work that is done for pay,"[5] something done for what a person could get out of it. Today this word has found its way into our political jargon as "partisanship" and means the attitude of those who work only for their own interests and not for the interests of anyone else. Selfish ambition plots, connives and schemes and will use any means to gain its end. In the face of partisanship, Paul wrote, "Do nothing out of selfish ambition or vain conceit, but in humility consider others better than yourselves" (Philippians 2:3).

Have you ever known anyone possessing selfish ambition? There is a great deal of carnal promotion among God's people today. The spirit of selfish ambition has even infiltrated a number of churches. There was once love and unity in many churches until partisanship reared its ugly head. Remember, it does not come from God.

James astutely observed that selfish ambition and envy are harbored — anchored, settled in, given a place — in the hearts of those who rely on the wisdom of the world. "But if you harbor bitter envy and selfish ambition in your hearts, do not boast about it or deny the truth" (James 3:14).

Disorder is a third result of applying the wisdom of the world to our lives. The Greek word translated "disorder" in James 3:16 is ἀκαταστασία. The word is used five times in the New Testament and refers to commotion, confusion or strife. Ακαταστασία is "disorder caused by those who demand their own rights and exercise a party spirit."[6] Sometimes the word is translated "anarchy."

When men and women rely on the wisdom of the world, the results are envy and selfish ambition, which in turn lead to disorder. Pandemonium, confusion and disorder are the natural results when people are more interested in pursuing their own ambitions than in being open to God's spirit in order to edify the body of Christ. Instead of bringing people together, the wisdom of the world drives people apart. Instead of producing unity, it produces divisiveness.

Most of us have known people who were clever in worldly things. Perhaps they were skillful in speech, but their effect on a committee was to create envy, partisanship and disorder because their wisdom was rooted in the secular, the sensual and the Satanic. It is sobering to realize that while some of us think we are doing God's work, in reality we may be doing Satan's work.

The word translated "disorder" in James 3:16 is also used in 1 Corinthians 14:33. "God is not a God of disorder but of peace." Yes, God is not the author of confusion. Confusion is the natural result of a mentality that finds its wisdom in the world.

A fourth result of the wisdom of the world is perversion, which James 3:16 calls "every evil practice," φαῦλος. The Greek word means vile or foul, literally "good for nothing." The wisdom of the world is good for nothing. It brings about jealousy, strife, confusion and eventually every evil practice.

We do not have to teach our children the wisdom of the world. They are born with it. We are all born with the propensity for envy, partisanship, confusion and perversion. Did you ever have to teach your child to disobey or say no? Of course not. Did you ever have to teach your child to grab a toy from someone else? No. Did you ever have to teach your child to get into a group and exclude someone else? No. Did you ever have to teach your children to fight with their brothers and sisters? No. Did you have to teach your child to say something unkind or ugly about someone else? No. The wisdom of the world is inherited through our sin nature.

Why are some of us so surprised that jealousy eats at us like a cancer? Why are some of us so surprised that confusion reigns in our lives, in our homes or in our businesses? Why are some of us so surprised that lying, scheming and every evil practice have become a part of our lifestyles? We should not be surprised if we have been getting our wisdom from the world and not from the Word. Some of us are in trouble because we made major decisions on the basis of the wisdom of the world. The greatest need we have in our world today is wisdom from God.

II. The Wisdom of the Word
James 3:17–18

Its Origin

The "but" in James 3:17 is not there by accident. Having just dealt with the wisdom of the world, James wanted to contrast it with the wisdom of the Word. This godly wisdom, σοφία, is defined by John Blanchard as "the ability to discern God's hand in human circumstances and apply heavenly judgment to earthly situations."

The wisdom of the Word has a divine origin; it "comes from heaven" (James 3:17). Solomon said, "For the Lord gives wisdom, and from his mouth come knowledge and understanding" (Proverbs 2:6). Paul also knew the source, for he wrote, "I keep asking that the God of our Lord Jesus Christ, the glorious Father, may give you the Spirit of wisdom and revelation" (Ephesians 1:17). And he said, "We have not stopped praying for you and asking God to fill you with the knowledge of his will through all spiritual wisdom and understanding" (Colossians 1:9).

The wisdom of the Word is God's gift, supernaturally

bestowed to His people. James 1:5 tells us to ask God for the gift. We do not get God's wisdom from education or practical experience. It is not learned. It is a gift to us from God, who gives it generously when we ask. Remember, however, that James 1:6 tells us that we must ask in faith.

Godly wisdom is found in the Living Word, the Lord Jesus Christ. He is our wisdom. He is "the power of God and the wisdom of God. It is because of him that you are in Christ Jesus, who has become for us wisdom from God" (1 Corinthians 1:24, 30). Without the Living Word, the Lord Jesus Christ, we have no hope of gaining true wisdom. Consequently, the way to begin finding wisdom is to receive Him as Savior and Lord.

Godly wisdom is also found in the written Word, the Bible. Writing to Timothy, Paul said, "From infancy you have known the holy Scriptures, which are able to make you wise for salvation through faith in Christ Jesus" (2 Timothy 3:15). The wisdom of the Word originates with the Living Word and the written Word, and both are supernaturally given.

While vacationing in Colorado one summer, my wife and I met a lady whose husband pastored a local church. In passing conversation I asked where he had attended school. Rather smugly she replied, "The Holy Spirit is his teacher, and he doesn't need any formal education." Let me warn you that having the wisdom of the Word does not mean that you shouldn't study and obtain knowledge through education. Note that James 3:13 refers to both wisdom and understanding. Wisdom σοφία — is "the ability to discern from facts, a divine enduement." Understanding επιστημον — is "intellectual perception, the accumulation of facts," which implies knowledge acquired through human effort.

Some of us have knowledge (facts) and no wisdom (discernment). Some of us have wisdom and no knowledge. God is calling for balance. James 3:13 asks, "Who is wise *and* understanding among you?" *(italics added)* The intelligence of some people borders on genius, but they cannot practically manage their lives. Other people are discerning but do not apply themselves to gain knowledge. Some of us have little or no heavenly wisdom because we do not apply ourselves to study the Bible.

Knowledge, we recall, is the accumulation of facts, whereas wisdom is the ability to take the facts, deal with them and apply them to life's situations. It is hard to do what the Bible says if we do not know what it says. Asking for wisdom does not eliminate our need to study (2 Timothy 2:15 KJV). Wisdom and knowledge are inseparable. They go together like ham and eggs, steak and potatoes, and corn beef and cabbage.

Its Outcome

When we apply the wisdom of the Word to our lives, the first result is purity (James 3:17). The Greek word for "pure," ἁγνός, implies spiritual integrity.[7] It carries with it the connotation of being undefiled and morally blameless, the chastity of a virgin bride.[8] While the wisdom of the world results in perversion, the wisdom of the Word results in purity.

We do not become pure before God through our works or efforts. We become pure before God through His work at Calvary. The heart is made pure through the blood of the Lord Jesus Christ.

James was saying that if a person is not first pure, he will not have any of the other characteristics of true wisdom either: "Peace-loving, considerate, submissive, full of mercy and good fruit, impartial and sincere" (James 3:17). Being comes before doing. Many people are seeking to live in peace who have not first been made pure through the Lord Jesus Christ.

A pure person will be peace-loving. The Greek word for "peace-loving," εἰρηνικός, means "a promoter of peace." Jesus said, "Blessed are the peacemakers, for they will be called sons of God" (Matthew 5:9). Peace of heart grows out of purity of heart. Peace does not come before purity. Purity must come before peace.

The Word's wisdom produces right relationships in the upward expression (peace with God), in the inward expression (peace with ourselves) and in the outward expression (peace with others). We will never enjoy peace with others until we are at peace with ourselves, and we will never be at peace with ourselves until we are at peace with God. The world's wisdom brings competition, conflict and confusion. The wisdom of the Word brings peace.

Still another result of applying the Word's wisdom is patience. James 3:17 uses three words to characterize patience: "considerate, submissive and merciful." Let's look at each of these three words in more detail.

First, the patience that results from the Word's wisdom is considerate. The Greek word for "considerate," ἐπιεικής, means "kind, willing to yield, steadfast humble patience." It is the exact opposite of the bitter envying that the world's wisdom produces.

Second, the patience that results from the Word's wisdom is "submissive" (εὐπειθής). A person who has the wisdom of the Word not only knows how to lead, but also knows how to follow. The Greek word εὐπειθής is used in the New Testament only in James 3:17. Here it means "willing to yield" and is the opposite of being disobedient or having selfish ambition. Εὐπειθής is a military word used to describe submission to military discipline, submission to authority. The submissive man is not stubborn or autocratic. He is open to discussion and negotiation.

Third, the patience that results from the Word's wisdom is "merciful" (ἔλεος). A merciful person knows how to deal with interpersonal relationships. Jesus said, "Blessed are the merciful, for they will be shown mercy" (Matthew 5:7). God's wisdom always results in forgiveness. Although it takes two to start a quarrel, it only takes one to stop it.

The wisdom of the Word has its origin in God and results in purity, peace, patience and productivity. James 3:17 says that godly wisdom is full of good fruit. While the wisdom of the world results in perversion, the wisdom of the Word results in productivity. A citrus farmer plants orange trees for the express purpose of harvesting oranges. So should it be with Christians. Faithful folks are fruitful folks. Show me someone who is pure in heart, peace-loving and patient, and I will show you someone who is productive. There is a chain reaction.

In contrast, the wisdom of the world with its roots in the secular, sensual and Satanic sows seeds of discord in the church. The harvest is envy, partisanship, confusion and perversion. Seeds of righteousness can never be grown in such soil and, consequently, they produce no lasting fruit.

Jesus reminds us that His disciples will be known "by their fruit" (Matthew 7:20). When I think of the result of the Word's wisdom, I think of the first Christian martyr, Stephen. Luke recorded: "Now Stephen, a man full of God's grace and power, did great wonders and miraculous signs among the people. Opposition arose, however, from members of the Synagogue of the Freedmen (as it was called) — Jews of Cyrene and Alexandria as well as the provinces of Cilicia and Asia. These men began to argue with Stephen, but they could not stand up against his wisdom or the Spirit by whom he spoke" (Acts 6:8–10).

The wisdom of the Word can change your life. It can make you pure, peace-loving, patient, productive and prudent. While the wisdom of the world results in partisanship (the party spirit), the wisdom of the Word results in prudence that is characterized by impartiality and sincerity (James 3:17).

The word "impartial" in James 3:17 is derived from the Greek word ἀδιάκριτος, which just appears this one time in the New Testament and means "the opposite of exhibiting prejudice, not divided." Ἀδιάκριτος is the opposite of doubting or wavering. When a man trusts in the world's wisdom, he feels pressure from one side and then another to change his viewpoint. For example, we have all known politicians who switched their stands on major issues, who flip-flopped for political expediency. When we have the wisdom of the Word, however, we can be decisive and not afraid. We can be impartial. The wisdom that comes from God does not play favorites with either the rich or the poor. Godly prudence does not favor one social group above another or one color above another.

This prudence is also characterized by sincerity. In James 3:17 the Greek word for "sincere," ἀνυπόκριτος, literally means "no hypocrisy." The Word's wisdom is without hypocrisy.

A form of hypocrisy was characteristic of ancient Greek drama. One actor would take on two or three roles in the same play. While on stage, he would hold several different masks. When it was time for one character to speak, the actor would put that particular mask in front of his face. The actor would then change to another character and put a different mask in front of his face. In some instances, the actor would be both hero and villain in the same play! Such an actor was called in the Greek world a "hypocrite." Over the years, this word found its way into our religious vernacular and now describes a two-faced individual who hides behind the mask of a false life. A hypocrite pretends to be something that he is not. James was saying that true wisdom does not hide behind a mask, pretending to be something it is not.

The wisdom of the Word is sincere. The wisdom of the Word is our greatest need — as persons, as providers, as partners, as parents. How can we get such wisdom? Solomon said, "The fear of the Lord is the beginning of knowledge [wisdom], but fools despise wisdom and discipline. My son, if you accept my words and store up my commands within you, turning your ear to wisdom and applying your heart to understanding, and if you call out for insight and cry aloud for understanding, and if you look for it as for silver and search for it as for hidden treasure, then you will understand the fear of the Lord and find the knowledge of God" (Proverbs 1:7; 2:1–5).

We each must choose between the wisdom of the world and the wisdom of the Word. One kind of wisdom finds its origin in the secular, sensual and Satanic; the other kind of wisdom finds its origin in Heaven. One results in envy, partisanship, confusion and perversion. The other results in purity, peace, patience, productivity and prudence. The choice is ours. The wisest decision we could ever make is to say an eternal yes to the Lord Jesus Christ.

❈ CHAPTER EIGHT ❈

WAR AND PEACE
JAMES 4:1–12

I. War Has Its Symptoms (James 4:1–3)
II. War Has Its Sources (James 4:4–6)
III. War Has Its Solutions (James 4:7–12)

"What causes fights and quarrels among you?" (James 4:1) Our current world situation makes James' opening question as relevant in our day as in any previous generation. War has been a part of every era of human history. No civilization has been immune to it. Our Lord spoke of "wars and rumors of wars" (Matthew 24:6). During the past 500 years, Great Britain alone has been engaged in nearly 80 major wars. During its relatively brief life span, the United States has taken part in at least 15 major wars. In nearly 5,600 years of recorded history, approximately 15,000 wars have been fought. This is an average of almost three wars every year. War is a way of life for those of us who live on planet earth. And as General Sherman, the Union leader who burned Confederate cities on his march to the sea, said, "War is hell!"

Critical days lie before us. Even though the Berlin wall has crumbled and the cold war seems to have subsided, our world may be closer than ever to global war.

The continuing Middle Eastern conflict cannot be settled at negotiating tables. The roots of the conflict are firmly embedded in centuries of ethnic hatred and hostility that are finally reaching the boiling point. Middle Eastern Bedouins no longer ride camels and shoot single-shot rifles. Today they drive tanks, fly supersonic fighter planes and wear body bombs. Many of them do this in the spirit of a jihad — a holy war. It is no coincidence that events that may be leading up to Armageddon are transpiring in the exact geographical spot foretold by the Biblical prophets thousands of years ago.

The Bible tells us that in the last days there will be an escalation of wars, eventually culminating in a final climactic battle — Armageddon. The stage may well be being set. Many people believe that the curtain is about to rise on the final act of mankind. A world on the brink of apocalyptic war should heed the words of James. He revealed that war has its symptoms, its sources and its solutions.

Perhaps some of us are at war right now. Oh, we are not dressed in battle fatigues, sitting in armored tanks in a Middle Eastern desert, but we may be at war. Some of us are at war with ourselves, as our flesh wars against the spirit. Others of us are at war in our homes. Some of us are even at war with God. What causes these fights and quarrels?

I. War Has Its Symptoms
James 4:1–3

There is a vast difference between symptoms and sources. For example, we do not get over a flu virus (the source of illness) by simply treating a runny nose (the symptom). James 4:11 talks about a symptom: "Brothers, do not slander one another." The believers to whom James was writing were engaged in a personal war of words. Their words were an external symptom, not the cause of their fighting.

Why are we at war with each other? We are at war with each other because we are at war with ourselves. The war of words is not the real problem. The real problem is within. So James astutely asked a second question: "Don't they come from your desires that battle within you?" (James 4:1).

In many ways, a Christian is a civil war incarnate. Paul put it like this: "The sinful nature desires what is contrary to the Spirit, and the Spirit what is contrary to the sinful nature. They are in conflict with each other, so that you do not do what you want" (Galatians 5:17). The Greek word translated "desires," ἡδονή, is the word from which we derive the English word "hedonism." This Greek word is "an unbridled search for pleasure." It is the spirit that demands immediate selfish satisfaction.[1] It has to do with pleasing oneself at the expense of others and is the plague of the western world.

For many people, life has become a competitive arena. An insatiable desire for possessions, power, popularity, position and passion has begun to take over and such selfishness can lead to many wrongs. It can lead us to do wrong things such as "kill and covet" (James 4:2). It can lead us to refrain from asking for the right things: "You do not have, because you do not ask God" (4:2). It can lead us to ask with the wrong motives: "When you ask, you do not receive, because you ask with wrong motives, that you may spend what you get on your pleasures" (4:3). If we never ask or if we ask with wrong motives, our prayer lives can become futile.

All war finds its origin in selfish desire. It does not matter whether it is global war, regional war, gang war, family war or cold war. Selfish desire is always at its root. As James 4:2 says, "You want something but don't get it." Our English word "want" is a translation of the Greek ἐπιθυμέω, which means "a longing to possess, a yearning or passion for something." Paul used the same word in Titus 3:3 to indicate that we can become slaves to our passions: "At one time we too were foolish, disobedient, deceived and enslaved by all kinds of passions and pleasures. We lived in malice and envy, being hated and hating one another."

We always want what we cannot have. Sometimes we even

want what belongs to someone else — his job, or his land or his wife. This "wanting" is never satisfied. I could ask most of the wealthiest men in my city, "How much is enough?" and the answer would be, "Just a little more." Worldly things never bring permanent satisfaction.

It is this selfish desire within that causes war with others. It is the very thing that motivates an Adolf Hitler or a Saddam Hussein. It is a desire to rule, to control. We need to remember that war is simply an external symptom and not a source. The source is within us. Every outward belligerent action is an eruption, a symptom of an inward selfish desire. The outward sins of David and Bathsheba that eventually resulted in murder began with his selfish desire to have someone who belonged to someone else. The six million innocent Jews annihilated in Nazi ovens were but the outward symptom of Hitler's inward selfish desire for power. Yes, our fights and quarrels come from our desires that battle within us.

II. War Has Its Sources
James 4:4–6

The source of war is not found in our relationship with others or in our relationship with ourselves. The source of war is found in our rebellious relationship with God. James called this conflict between man and God a "battle within" (James 4:1). Στρατεύω, the Greek verb for "I battle," means "to carry on a campaign." In this battle, a rebellious man constantly fights to have his own way. His selfish desires continually war against the Spirit. Rebellion against God is the root cause of every war — in the home, in the heart or on the battlefield.

James 4:4 says, "Anyone who chooses to be a friend of the world becomes an enemy of God." The Greek word translated "world," κόσμος literally means "a human society apart from God."[2] The world's prevailing system of thought is anti-God and anti-Christ. Thus, whenever we are not on guard spiritually, we can very subtly become a "friend" (φιλία) of the world; that is, we can have "an affection for it or a liking to be with it." Some Christians, for example, like to be among worldly things that God says we should avoid.

Friendship with the world will ultimately lead us toward a love of the world. First John 2:15 warns, "Do not love the world or anything in the world. If anyone loves the world, the love of the Father is not in him." Don't be mistaken; there is no demilitarized zone for Christians who are out of fellowship with God. If you are a friend of the world, you are an enemy of God. There is no "no man's land." James 4:4 declares, "You adulterous people, don't you know that friendship with the world is hatred toward God?" Don't be like Demas who deserted Paul "because he loved this world" (2 Timothy 4:10).

Our world is repulsed by the antics of such men as Saddam Hussein. This dictator reportedly murdered cabinet members as well as family members. He used poison gas on some of his own people. He plundered a sovereign nation, burned its oil fields and held innocent civilians hostage, threatening to use them as human shields. However, as we think of this evil man, we need to remember that potentially there is a Saddam Hussein within each of us. War comes from the desires that battle within us.

The phrase "adulterous people" in James 4:4 is feminine in the Greek. Was James singling out only women here? Are not men guilty too? James used the feminine because he was talking about the "bride" of Christ. Paul was speaking of the church as the bride of Christ when he wrote: "I am jealous for you with a godly jealousy. I promised you to one husband, to Christ, so that I might present you as a pure virgin to him" (2 Corinthians 11:2). James was referring to all Christians who commit spiritual adultery. In the Old Testament, the entire book of Hosea is consumed with the thought of spiritual adultery. And Jeremiah, speaking for God, said, "Like a woman unfaithful to her husband, so you have been unfaithful to me, O house of Israel" (Jeremiah 3:20).

Are any of us guilty of spiritual adultery? We once came to an altar and made a pledge, openly and publicly, to Christ. We should have been as true to God as a faithful woman is true to her husband. But in becoming friends with the world, some of us have climbed into bed with other gods, perhaps the gods of materialism or popularity. When we began to desire worldly things more than God, we committed spiritual adultery. We are like married women who go after other men, flirting and seducing them.

Spiritual adultery was the sin of the church at Ephesus to whom Jesus said, "I hold this against you: You have forsaken your first love. Remember the height from which you have fallen! Repent and do the things you did at first" (Revelation 2:4–5). Jesus did not say that these folks had "lost" their first love, but that they had "left" (forsaken) their first love. To continue this beautiful image, we have a loving and faithful husband in the Lord Jesus Christ. Why are we at war with Him who seeks only our best interests and will protect and provide for us?

I do not believe James was speaking softly here. I think he was shouting and pounding his pulpit! He was expressing surprise and shock because those who had claimed to know Christ for years had committed spiritual adultery. "What has happened to you?" he was saying. "Where is your wisdom in knowing right from wrong? Have you lost your sense of moral values? Don't you know?"

The Greeks used at least two words that we translate into our English word "know." One is γινωσκω, which means "to know by observation and experience." The other is οιδα which means "to know by reflection."[3] James 4:4 uses οιδα to show that we do not have to experience a certain sin to know that it is wrong. We know by reflection. God gave us the capacity to reflect on His goodness and to know right from wrong.

God also gives us the strength or grace to resist the temptation to do what we know is wrong. James 4:6 says, "But he gives us more grace." This is the most beautiful verse in James' entire letter. Though often overlooked, it is relevant today. Annie Johnson Flint came close to capturing the thought in her song:

He giveth more grace when the burden grows greater;
He sendeth more strength when the labors increase.
To added affliction He addeth His mercy;
To multiplied trials, His multiplied peace.

When we have exhausted our store of endurance,
When our strength has failed ere the day is half done,
When we reach the end of our hoarded resources,
Our Father's full giving is only begun.

His love has no limit; His grace has no measure;
His pow'r has no boundary known unto men.
For out of His infinite riches in Jesus,
He giveth, and giveth, and giveth again!

III. War Has Its Solutions
James 4:7–12

God has given us the solution to war in the Lord Jesus Christ. Whether it be a cosmic conflict or a family fight, there is but one true and eternal solution to war. There will never be peace without the Prince of Peace. This sounds simplistic, but it is true. History continues to testify to wars and rumors of more wars, but one day Christ will come again to usher in a millennium of peace when swords will be beaten into plowshares and the lion will lie down with the lamb.

There will never be international peace until we have peace on a national level. There will never be peace on a national level until it exists on a state level. There will never be peace on a state level until it is found on a county level. There will never be peace on a county level until it is found on the city level. There will never be peace on a city level until there is peace in our neighborhoods. There will never be peace in our neighborhoods until there is peace on each street. There will never be peace on each street until there is peace on each block. There will never be peace on our blocks until there is peace in our homes. There will never be peace in our homes until there is peace in our own hearts through personal faith in Jesus Christ. Therefore, the only real and lasting solution for war, whether it be abroad or in our hearts, is an eternal solution.

James concluded this discussion on war with a series of verbs, all of which are in the imperative. These commands are five steps toward peace. James' pathway to peace is found in these verbs: submit, resist, come near, wash, humble yourselves. Peace, he was saying, is found in submission, opposition, proposition, admonition and disposition.

Step One: Submission

James 4:7 says, "Submit yourselves, then, to God. Resist the devil, and he will flee from you." Many Christians who read this verse rush out to resist the devil and succumb to him every time. Why? The resistance James mentioned has a prerequisite. We are first to submit ourselves to God and then resist the devil.

The Greek word for "submit," ὑποτάσσω, means "to obey." *This word* comes from two Greek words meaning "under" and "to place oneself." James was saying that we are to put ourselves under the lordship of Jesus Christ. James uses ὑποτάσσω here to illustrate with a military term that compels one to get into his proper rank. Warren Wiersbe pointed out that "when a buck private begins to try and act like a general, there is going to be trouble." Submission is the first step toward a solution to war.

After King David sinned with Bathsheba, he hid himself for almost a year. He was at war, experiencing an inner conflict with God. David referred to this conflict in Psalm 32:1–5 "Blessed is he whose transgressions are forgiven, whose sins are covered. Blessed is the man whose sin the Lord does not count against him and in whose spirit is no deceit. When I kept silent, my bones wasted away through my groaning all day long. For day and night your hand was heavy upon me; my strength was sapped as in the heat of summer. Then I acknowledged my sin to you and did not cover up my iniquity. I said, 'I will confess my transgressions to the Lord' — and you forgave the guilt of my sin." When David finally submitted, his war was replaced with peace.

Most of our problems can be traced to our refusal to submit to the lordship of Jesus Christ in every area of our lives. The first step toward resolving our inner conflicts is to submit to God.

Step Two: Opposition

God challenges us to oppose evil. When we submit to the Lord Jesus Christ, we get a new enemy, Satan. But we can resist him (James 4:7). The Greek word we translate "resist," ἀνθίστημι, comes from two words that mean "against" and "to stand." It is a military word meaning "to take your stand against." For example, allied troops "took their stand" on the Saudi Arabian–Kuwaiti border during the Persian Gulf War.

James was revealing to us that defensive warfare, not offensive warfare, is at issue here. We are to resist. Paul also referred to resistance: "Put on the full armor of God, so that when the day of evil comes, you may be able to stand your ground, and after you have done everything, to stand. Stand firm then, with the belt of truth buckled around your waist, with the breastplate of righteousness in place" (Ephesians 6:13–14).

Some of us have done the reverse. Instead of submitting to the Lord and resisting the devil, we have submitted to the devil and resisted God. When we come to temptation's corner, conflict ensues as the flesh works against the Spirit. God says, "Turn right; don't go to the left." Satan says, "Turn left; many are going this way." And we turn left. No wonder war rages within our hearts.

· Satan desires to keep us at war with God. Satan knows that if we ever submit to the lordship of Jesus Christ, we will declare war on him. Consequently, he appeals to our pride and sense of self-importance to keep us from humbling ourselves before God, just as he did in the Garden of Eden: "You will be like God" (Genesis 3:5). Satan also used this appeal to tempt Christ. What was Satan's strategy? He did not tempt Christ to kill, steal or commit adultery. He appealed to His pride. He took Him to a high mountain and to the pinnacle of the temple.

Many of us are fooled by this deceiver. Satan is not our problem; we are. But when we submit and resist, Satan will flee from us. Do we believe that?

Satan has already been defeated. First John 4:4 says, "You, dear children, are from God and have overcome them [evil spirits], because the one who is in you is greater than the one who is in the world." While Satan may be a roaring lion, that's all he can do — roar. He has no teeth! Peter said, "Be self-controlled and alert. Your enemy the devil prowls around like a roaring lion looking for someone to devour. Resist him, standing firm in the faith, because you know that your brothers throughout the world are undergoing the same kind of sufferings" (1 Peter 5:8–9). Satan's doom is sealed (Revelation 20:10–15). He has no authority, and Jesus has all authority. The only authority Satan has is what we yield to him when we are not submitted to the Lord Jesus Christ. When we submit to Christ and resist the devil, we will have taken the first two steps toward inner peace.

Step Three: Proposition

Following his challenge to resist Satan, James made an interesting proposition: "Come near to God and he will come near to you" (James 4:8). What a privilege it is to come near to God. There is only one way we can come near to God — through the blood of Jesus Christ. Paul said, "In Christ Jesus you who once were far away have been brought near through the blood of Christ" (Ephesians 2:13). That is why Christ came to earth. "Christ died for [our] sins once for all, the righteous for the unrighteous, to bring you to God" (1 Peter 3:18).

James was not referring to salvation here, since he was communicating with those he called "brothers." He was emphasizing the need of those Christians who are sinning and double-minded to repent (James 4:8). He was addressing those who are pulled and torn between the wisdom of the world and the wisdom of the Word.

The prodigal son in Luke 15 took these first three steps toward peace. First, he submitted to his father. In effect, he said to himself, "I will go back home. I have sinned, but I will get back under my father's authority." Then he took the second step. He took a stand against the devil. He turned his back on Satan and all of his enticements. Finally, he took the third step.

He accepted the proposition to draw near. He left the far country and went home. And as he neared home, what happened? His father saw him and ran to meet him. Likewise, if we draw near to God, He will come near to us.

Step Four: Admonition

The fourth step in resolving inner conflict is to admit our need and ask for forgiveness. "Wash your hands, you sinners, and purify your hearts, you double-minded. Grieve, mourn and wail. Change your laughter to mourning and your joy to gloom" (James 4:8–9). Only by confessing our sin and asking for forgiveness can we come near. "If we confess our sins, he is faithful and just and will forgive us our sins and purify us from all unrighteousness" (1 John 1:9).

Repentance is the issue here. James was referring to our repentance from external actions ("wash your hands") and from internal attitudes ("purify your hearts"). Jesus says that the actions of our hands are a result of the attitudes of our hearts. There are two things we need: clean hands and pure hearts. "Who may ascend the hill of the Lord?…He who has clean hands and a pure heart" (Psalm 24:3–4).

The mark of genuine repentance is deep, heartfelt sorrow for our sinful actions and attitudes (James 4:9). Repentance is not simply remorse or regret, though it involves both. Paul said, "Godly sorrow brings repentance that leads to salvation and leaves no regret, but worldly sorrow brings death" (2 Corinthians 7:10). There must be brokenness on our part, not just a casual, lackadaisical attitude toward sin. The prodigal said, "I am no longer worthy to be called your son" (Luke 15:19). He went home broken and thereby became, once again, an honored son.

Step Five: Disposition

After declaring our need to submit, resist, come near and wash, James said, "Humble yourselves before the Lord, and he will lift you up" (James 4:10). The Greek command to be humble, ταπεινω, means "to make low." The passive voice used by James indicates that the subject doesn't act but is indeed acted upon. The command is not to attempt to humble ourselves, but to allow God to work within us to make us humble. To humble ourselves before the Lord is to recognize our bankrupt spiritual condition and to admit our need of Him. The despised tax collector humbled himself when he went to the temple to pray and called out to God for mercy. Jesus said, "I tell you that this man, rather than the other [Pharisee], went home justified before God. For everyone who exalts himself will be humbled, and he who humbles himself, will be exalted" (Luke 18:14). It is so much better to humble ourselves than to be humbled.

James 4:6 says, "God opposes the proud but gives grace to the humble." The Greek word translated "opposes," ἀντιτάσσω, is a military term that literally means "to battle against." Yes, God battles against proud people. War with others or with ourselves is only a symptom of conflict between us and God. God battles against the proud. God hates the sin of pride (Proverbs 6:16–17).

But those who humble themselves will be lifted up by God. James 4:10 promises, "He will lift you up." How much better it is when Christ exalts us before others than when we seek to exalt ourselves before others. James was trying to show us that the way up is down. When we humble ourselves, He will exalt us. Is there anyone reading these words in need of being lifted up?

The words of Charles H. Gabriel's hymn may be for you:

In loving kindness Jesus came
My soul in mercy to reclaim,
And from the depths of sin and shame
Thro' grace He lifted me.

He called me long before I heard,
Before my sinful heart was stirred,
But when I took Him at His word,
Forgiv'n He lifted me.

Now on a higher plane I dwell,
And with my soul I know 'tis well;
Yet how or why, I cannot tell,
He should have lifted me.

From sinking sand He lifted me,
With tender hand He lifted me,
From shades of night to plains of light,
O praise His name, He lifted me!

If we would but follow the eternal solution — submit, resist, come near, wash, humble ourselves — our wars would cease. We would not be at war with God, and consequently we would not be at war with ourselves, which means we would not be at war with others. There can be no peace without the Prince of Peace.

War and peace are two of the great issues facing the church as it ministers in the third millennium and awaits the coming holocaust. Wars will continue to escalate as we head toward Armageddon. We need to remember, however, that God has not abdicated His throne. He is at work in history, and Biblical prophecy underscores the significance of modern events. Our God is the God of history, and in the midst of this cosmic chaos, He calls us to be peacemakers. We know the solution to war. We have the message of hope and the message of peace, and we must keep telling the story.

....
✸ CHAPTER NINE ✸
....

ROOTS OF RECESSION:
THE ARROGANCE OF THE AGE
JAMES 4:13–17

I. Foolish Presumptions (James 4:13,16)
II. Forgotten Perspectives (James 4:14)
III. Forsaken Priorities (James 4:15,17)

Recession! The word sends chills up the businessman's back. I asked several brokers and bankers to give me a one-sentence definition of this recurring dilemma of our western economy. One man replied, "A recession is two consecutive down quarters in the gross national product." Another elaborated, "A recession is an economic decline brought about by higher unemployment, declining consumer purchasing, tightening credit and an overall slump in the economy." Yet another answered, "It's a consistent decline in overall economic activity resulting in the loss of jobs." A fourth person said, "Recession is when your neighbor is out of work; depression is when you are out of work." Webster defined recession as "a period of reduced economic activity; a receding; a withdrawal."

Many people blame recession on budget deficits or the President of the United States. Others blame Congress, the financial scandals, the Middle Eastern oil crisis or management. Still others blame unions. If we ask a dozen men or women what brings on recession, we'll most likely receive a dozen different answers. Perhaps the real answer, as we'll shortly see, lies at the feet of many of us.

Sometime ago I awoke in the middle of the night feeling nauseous. I stumbled into the bathroom and flipped on the light. Opening the bathroom closet, I shuffled through the medicine drawer searching for something to calm my stomach. In the back of the drawer was a bottle of pink medicine. As I was about to take a dose, I suddenly noticed the big red letters on the side of the bottle: "SHAKE WELL BEFORE USING." I had to shake the bottle because the best part of the medicine had settled on the bottom and that which was less important in the healing process had risen to the top.

This simple illustration shows how proper priorities in our lives sometimes sink to the bottom, and other things rise to the top. And so, every once in a while, God has to write across our lives, "SHAKE WELL BEFORE USING." Days of recession, when we are being shaken, are not all bad. In times of recession we "cut out the fat." We get rid of excess baggage and cut our budgets. We get back to basics and put priorities in order.

James was less interested in an economic recession than in the spiritual recession plaguing many homes and hearts. Remember, a recession is defined as "a withdrawal, a period of reduced activity." The roots of spiritual recession are the same as the roots of economic recession. According to James 4:13–17, the roots of recession are threefold: foolish presumptions, forgotten perspectives and forsaken priorities.

James began this passage with the words, "Now listen." The verb is in the second-person singular, indicating that James was addressing each of us individually. He was saying: "I'm not talking to the congregation. I'm talking to you personally. Stop thinking that this chapter is for someone else. That is arrogance and presumption." Once James had his readers' attention, he revealed the roots of recession — the arrogance of our age.

1. Foolish Presumptions
James 4:13, 16

The man described in James 4:13 lives as if tomorrow will never come. He is obsessed with making money. Materialism is his master. The world's wealth is his only concern. His entire life is motivated by money and greed. He is a picture of a successful young business person. He isn't bad. There is nothing to indicate that he is unethical or unprofessional. He plans ahead and is self-confident, goal-oriented and profit-motivated. However, he lives life as a practical atheist with no consideration of God in his planning. He is the epitome of the "I can do it on my own" philosophy. This man in James 4:13 is a microcosm of American mentality.

Most employers would certainly like to have employees like this man. I like him myself. For him, failure is not a possibility; it's not even in his vocabulary. I like that. The Bible never condemns good planning, positive attitudes or hard work. And it doesn't here. His attitude is at issue here, not his actions. Note that James said, "You who *say*..." (James 4:13, *italics added*).

Here James switched to the second-person plural. He was making the point that although he was speaking to each of us individually, we each have plenty of company in the category of those who make their plans without God — those who live by foolish presumptions. The man James described is typical. In his arrogance, he presumes a lot of things. "As it is, you boast and brag," said James. "All such boasting is evil" (James 4:16).

In arrogance, this man presumes the when — the duration. He says, "Today or tomorrow" (James 4:13). Now there is nothing wrong with planning ahead, but he leaves a key element out of his plans. He ought to say, "If it is the Lord's will, we will live and do this or that" (4:15). In arrogance, he also presumes the where — the location. He says, "I'll go to this city." There is nothing wrong with positive thinking. The problem is that he once again has left out the will of the Lord. In arrogance, he also presumes the what — the vocation. He says, "I'll carry on business." There is nothing wrong with being goal-oriented, but he has still left God out of his plans. Finally, he arrogantly presumes the why — the motivation. His underlying motivation is to "make money" (4:13). There is nothing wrong with being profit-motivated, but he has still not considered the will of the Lord.

The When, the Duration

In arrogance people can make the foolish presumption that their time will not run out. Men and women at staff meetings discuss timetables. They plan to "clean up" within a year, forgetting that God's timing may be different. Jesus told a parable that illustrates their foolishness. The parable is recorded in Luke 12:16–26:

> *The ground of a certain rich man produced a good crop. He thought to himself, "What shall I do? I have no place to store my crops?"*
>
> *Then he said, "This is what I'll do. I will tear down my barns and build bigger ones, and there I will store all my grain and my goods. And I'll say to myself, 'You have plenty of good things laid up for many years. Take life easy; eat, drink and be merry.'"*
>
> *But God said to him, "You fool! This very night your life will be demanded from you. Then who will get what you have prepared for yourself?"*
>
> *This is how it will be with anyone who stores up things for himself but is not rich toward God.*
>
> *Then Jesus said to his disciples: "Therefore I tell you, do not worry about your life, what you will eat; or about your*

body, what you will wear. Life is more than food, and the body more than clothes. Consider the ravens: They do not sow or reap, they have no storeroom or barn; yet God feeds them. And how much more valuable you are than birds! Who of you by worrying can add a single hour to his life? Since you cannot do this very little thing, why do you worry about the rest?"

Talk about a smashing success! This man had a bumper crop, so he decided to build bigger barns and have greater security for the future. He wanted to possess more and more. He is like many men and women who sit in their easy chairs with a false sense of security based on a foolish presumption.

Like the rich man in the parable, many of us become so consumed in our work that we forget that we have a spiritual dimension as well as a physical one. We must not be fooled into believing that there will always be adequate time to get our houses in order. We must not live by foolish presumptions.

James 4:14 says, "You do not even know what will happen tomorrow. What is your life? You are a mist that appears for a little while and then vanishes." Every day we can pick up the newspaper and read the obituary column. Sometimes people we know are listed there. Some were strong and healthy and last week told us about their future plans. They told us how they were going to buy and sell, but death interrupted their plans. Life here on earth is but a mist. We must not make foolish presumptions that exclude God. Businessmen and women do well to look into the future. The problem is they often don't look far enough into the future. Some people who pride themselves in being goal-oriented simply do not look far enough ahead; they stop too soon. Many make presumptions about the duration of life on earth. But God says, "Do not boast about tomorrow, for you do not know what a day may bring forth" (Proverbs 27:1).

The Where, the Location

In arrogance people can make foolish presumptions about where they should go. Picture again a staff meeting where men and women are in a strategy session. Their maps are stretched out on the conference table. They discuss population trends, trade routes and the growth potential of various cities. They draw their conclusions, but they forget that God's ideas may be different from theirs.

Jonah made some foolish presumptions regarding the where, the location. God had called him to go to Nineveh and be the agent of a great spiritual revival, but the Bible says that "Jonah ran away from the Lord and headed for Tarshish" (Jonah 1:3). God's will for Jonah's life was Nineveh. However, he thought it best to go in the opposite direction toward Tarshish. He thought he had it all figured out.

Jonah's foolish presumption caused him to fall. He went down to Joppa. He went down into the ship. He went down into the sea. He went down into the fish's belly. Anyone who lives his life on the basis of foolish presumptions is ultimately dragged down. Once a person steps on the pathway of disobedience to God, the road keeps spiraling downward. No one ever goes up when he lives in rebellion against God. We don't fall up; we fall down.

Jonah's fall was costly. The Bible says that he paid the fare to Tarshish, but the rest of his story reveals that his trip was much more expensive than he ever dreamed it would be. I have seen many people who have paid the fare of life because of foolish presumptions. Living by foolish presumptions can be costly. Sometimes the most expensive thing a person ever does is run from God's will.[1]

The What, the Vocation

In arrogance, people can make foolish presumptions about what they should do. Those men and women in the staff meeting decide to obliterate the competition to close the deal, ask for the sale, get the business. They forget that God may have a different vocation in mind for them.

Saul of Tarsus was en route to Damascus to do some planned terrorist business. He planned to beat up some Christians and imprison them. He had it all figured out — the when, the where, the what and even the why. He actually thought he was doing God a service and that God would be pleased. However, God had other plans for him. God had another job for him to do. So God confronted Saul on the Damascus road; He knocked him off his horse and completely transformed his life. Saul became the great Apostle Paul and lived the rest of his days with this addendum tacked on to his life: "If it be the Lord's will..."

The Why, the Motivation

In arrogance people can allow foolish motivations to control their actions. Back in that boardroom, we look into the faces of those who sit around the table to read their motives. Apparently, their chief desire is to make "just a little more" for the bottom line. Presumptuous as they are, they do not carry on their business for the purpose of giving glory to the Lord.

Elisha's trusted companion Gehazi acted on a foolish presumption. Naaman, the commander-in-chief of the Syrian army, had just been cured of leprosy and had returned to Elisha to offer him money and thanksgiving. Elisha flatly refused, reminding Naaman that God's cure for sin cannot be purchased, that it is the free gift of God. Gehazi silently watched the whole scene unfold. Second Kings 5:20–22 says:

> *Gehazi, the servant of Elisha the man of God, said to himself, "My master was too easy on Naaman, this Aramean, by not accepting from him what he brought. As surely as the Lord lives, I will run after him and get something from him."*
>
> *So Gehazi hurried after Naaman. When Naaman saw him running toward him, he got down from the chariot to meet him. "Is everything all right?" he asked.*
>
> *"Everything is all right," Gehazi answered. "My master sent me to say, 'Two young men from the company of the prophets have just come to me from the hill country of Ephraim. Please give them a talent of silver and two sets of clothing.'"*

But these were all lies. Because he was motivated by making money, Gehazi met his fate. Second Kings 5:25–27 records:

> *Then he went in and stood before his master Elisha.*
> *"Where have you been, Gehazi?" Elisha asked.*
> *"Your servant didn't go anywhere," Gehazi answered.*
> *But Elisha said to him, "Was not my spirit with you when the man got down from his chariot to meet you? Is this the time to take money, or to accept clothes, olive groves, vineyards, flocks, herds, or menservants and maidservants? Naaman's leprosy will cling to you and to your descendants forever." Then Gehazi went from Elisha's presence and he was leprous, as white as snow.*

"Do not be deceived; God cannot be mocked. A man reaps what he sows" (Galatians 6:7).

What motivates you and me? There is nothing wrong with

being motivated to make a profit. In fact, Jesus told the parable of the talents to stress this very point. He wants His people to take certain risks. But the motive of Christian businessmen should be to glorify God in the process of making a profit. Our main motivation ought never to be simply making money. The heart of our motivation ought to be how we can use our income to further God's kingdom.

There is nothing wrong with making money, but a Christian should not want to make a profit by "hook or by crook." That would be a foolish presumption about motivation. Profits can be made without the Lord, but they often bring unhappiness, misery, heartbreak and heartache. A Christian could be the most profit-motivated person in his community, but he ought to want to make a profit in order to give glory to the Lord Jesus Christ; he ought to acquire and use resources according to God's will.

Some men and women not only allow foolish motivations to control their plans, but they also boast and brag about it. James 4:16 says, "As it is you boast and brag. All such boasting is evil." This verse reminds me of some bragging I encountered in 1972. That year my family and I moved to our first pastorate in Hobart, Oklahoma, a county seat of about 5,000 people in a wheat-farming area. Their only traffic light was on the town square by the courthouse. Opposite the courthouse was the drugstore with its old-fashioned fountain — the place to be seen in Hobart.

Now 1972 was not exactly the dark ages, but folks in that community used several old remedies. I still have a thin metal box of "Dr. Sparagus Kidney Pills" that I purchased out of curiosity and nostalgia in that drugstore. The words on the pillbox make quite a claim. They say that the pills "cure Bright's disease, diabetes, bladder troubles, cystitis, nephritis, sleeplessness, nervousness, congestion of the kidneys, blood troubles, gout, rheumatism, sallow complexion, anemia, chlorosis, nervous headache, dizziness, hysteria, neuralgia, etc." I suppose the thing that gets me the most is the "etc." That box of pills promised a great deal, but it couldn't deliver. This simple story illustrates the bragging that James said is evil.

The Greek word for "brag," ἀλαζονεία, means "a wanderer, a vagabond." It could describe a quack doctor in the nineteenth century who would pull his wagon into town and boast about his cure-alls and elixirs. He would sell them on the street from the side of his wagon and then slip out of town under the cover of darkness.

James said that people who leave God out of their lives are full of empty boasting. They talk big, but when it comes to the bottom line, they are like Dr. Sparagus Kidney Pills. They have nothing that can cure the sin-sick soul and bring peace, hope and healing. Even though their bank accounts may be bulging, they have a recession of the soul.

Was James saying that it is wrong to talk about the when, the where, the what and the why? No. Christians ought to be the best planners in their communities. It is not foolish to plan ahead, but it is foolish to plan ahead without God. It is good to have goals, but they will let us down if we leave God out of them.

James was warning us not to make foolish presumptions about the future, with no thought of God. This does not mean that those of us in business should be passive. If we are Christians, we ought to have positive attitudes. We ought to do more detailed growth planning than anyone else. We should be goal-oriented and profit-motivated because we have an edge. We have Someone on our side who knows best. God has a perfect plan for our lives and His timing is always best. He "is able to do immeasurably more than all we ask or imagine" (Ephesians 3:20). As Christians, however, we need to add this to our plans: "If it be the Lord's will." We are not to make foolish presumptions.

Many Christians are experiencing a recession of the soul —

a period of reduced spiritual activity. In the arrogance of our age, they presume they can grow in Christ when they want to, where they want to and how they want to. These are but foolish presumptions. Recession, whether it be economic or spiritual, is rooted in foolish presumptions and in forgotten perspectives.

II. Forgotten Perspectives
James 4:14

During the Persian Gulf War and Iraqi wars, our church sent thousands of camouflaged New Testaments to American troops in the Middle East. One night in a bunker in the Saudi desert, while artillery shells flew overhead, a young soldier took out one of those Bibles and read James 4:14: "Why, you do not even know what will happen tomorrow. What is your life? You are a mist that appears for a little while and then vanishes." The type of situation that soldier was in put life into a new perspective. So many of us read a verse like this and pass right over it because we have forgotten the proper perspectives on life.

For so many of us, proper views of life and death are forgotten perspectives. We live as though this life were all there is. We seek to camouflage the aging process and pretend it is not happening. We never want to think about death. We act as if we have 99-year leases on our bodies with options to renew. However, death is life's greatest certainty.

Life Has Its Uncertainties

James asked, "What is your life?" Secular scientists and philosophers cannot satisfactorily answer this question. As Christians, however, we know that life does not end when our physical bodies die. We will go on living after death. God has instilled within the soul of man a longing for another life. Even primitive people longed for this. That is why cavemen drew pictures depicting an afterlife. That is why Egyptians were buried with eating utensils, weapons, servants and horses. That is why the Indians believed in a happy hunting ground. It is amazing that so many men and women spend so much of their time trying to take care of their physical bodies that will only live for a few years, and largely ignore their spirits that will live forever.

Fifty years from now most of us will be living in either Heaven or Hell. Does the word Hell bother you? We could attend thousands of churches in the western world today and never hear the word. Jesus, however, taught more about Hell than He did about Heaven. It is better to be bothered now than to ignore the thought and be bothered with the reality forever.

Forgetting the proper perspectives on life and death and life after death, many of us live from year to year when we ought to be living from day to day.[2] We number our years at each birthday when God says we ought to be numbering our days. Psalm 90:12 says, "Teach us to number our days aright, that we may gain a heart of wisdom."

James 4:14 asks, "What is your life?" and answers, "You are a mist that appears for a little while and then vanishes." The Greek word for "mist," ἀτμίς, only appears two times in the New Testament. The other time it appears is in Acts 2:19 and there it is translated "smoke." Mist is here one moment and gone the next. It's like the steam coming out of the teakettle on the stove. I am reminded of the famous line in Shakespeare's Macbeth: "Out, out, brief candle! Life's but a walking shadow, a poor player that struts and frets his hour upon the stage, and then is heard no more."

The Bible uses many other metaphors to drive home the truth of life's brevity. First Chronicles 29:15 reminds us that "our days on earth are like a shadow." Job 7:7 says, "My life is but a breath." Job 9:25 says, "My days are swifter than a runner." Psalm 102:3 states, "My days vanish like smoke."

The moment we are born, we begin to die. We will all pass away if Jesus does not return first. I have stood at the caskets of hundreds of people who have died in all sorts of ways — some by disaster in wrecks and in wars, some by disease and decay. One way or another, death will claim the bodies of all except those Christians who will be delivered from their bodies at the rapture of the church.

The point is, the length of life is uncertain. No matter how long we live, life is short. Some of us are deceived into thinking that we will have a long time to advance in our professions, enjoy our loved ones and serve the Lord Jesus here. But we do not even know what will happen tomorrow. Therefore, we must live for Christ today.

Talking about the uncertainties of life, Proverbs 27:1 says, "Do not boast about tomorrow, for you do not know what a day may bring forth." And Psalm 39:4–6 says, "Show me, O Lord, my life's end and the number of my days; let me know how fleeting is my life. You have made my days a mere handbreadth; the span of my years is as nothing before you. Each man's life is but a breath. Man is a mere phantom as he goes to and fro: He bustles about, but only in vain; he heaps up wealth, not knowing who will get it."

Corrie Ten Boom said, "It is not the duration of life that is important, but the donation of life." How are you spending your life? Are you wasting your life or investing it? Some of us are so busy trying to make a living that we have forgotten to make a life. Is your life merely an existence? Jesus said, "The thief comes only to steal and kill and destroy; I have come that they may have life, and have it to the full" (John 10:10). Jesus came to give us fullness of life.

Life Has Its Certainties

If the uncertainty of life is its duration, the certainty of life is that it vanishes. Yet death is often a forbidden topic. Our culture busily tries to camouflage the aging process through plastic surgery, cosmetics and hair color. We constantly and frantically look for new miracle drugs that will give us another few years. Some people are even involved in cryonics. They freeze the body after death with the hope that in the future medical science will find a cure for the disease that caused the death and bring the frozen body back to life. However, nothing can keep us from our appointments with death. The Bible says that all of our days were numbered before there was one. Hebrews 9:27 says, "Man is destined to die once, and after that to face judgment."

Peter Marshall used to tell an Arabic fable that illustrates this certainty. A merchant in Baghdad sent his servant to the market. Before long the servant returned, white and trembling. In great agitation, he said to his master, "Down in the marketplace I was jostled by a woman in the crowd. When I turned around, I saw that it was Death that jostled me. She looked at me and made a threatening gesture. Please lend me a horse that I might hasten to Samarra and hide there so Death cannot find me."

The merchant loaned him a horse, and the servant galloped away in haste. Later the merchant went to the marketplace and saw Death standing in the crowd. He went over to her and asked, "Why did you frighten my servant this morning? Why did you make a threatening gesture?"

Death replied, "That was not a threatening gesture. I was only startled and surprised. I was astonished to see him in Baghdad, for I have an appointment with him tonight in Samarra."

Each of us has an appointment in Samarra. If we put our faith and trust in Christ, the One who holds the keys to death and Hell, this appointment should cause not fear but rejoicing. We have a hope, and it enables us to sing, "Because He lives I can face tomorrow!"[3] We are not ready to live until we are ready to die. This is why the call of Amos 4:12 comes thundering down through the corridors of the centuries: "Prepare to meet your God."

Economic or spiritual recession is rooted in foolish presumptions and forgotten perspectives. We have used a telescope to look at length upon foolish presumptions. We have used a periscope to come into closer range to examine forgotten perspectives. Now we will use a microscope in our study of recession, and we will see that it is also rooted in forsaken priorities.

III. Forsaken Priorities
James 4:15,17

The story is told of a man who was riding his motorcycle along a country road. He stopped to talk to a preacher in a churchyard. When the preacher inquired, the man indicated that he was going into town to sell his motorcycle. The preacher paraphrasing James 4:15 replied, "You ought to say, 'I am riding into town to sell my motorcycle if it be the Lord's will.'" The man rolled his eyes, laughed and mocked the preacher's words. Then he roared off down the two-lane country highway on his motorcycle.

Late that afternoon the preacher was sitting on his front porch just before the sun went down. He looked down the long road and saw a man stumbling and staggering from one side of the road to the other. As the preacher stood up, he recognized the friend with whom he had talked earlier in the day. The knees of his friend's pants were torn open exposing skinned legs. His arm was in a makeshift sling. His shirt was half torn off his back. His face was swollen and black and blue. His hair was a mess. His elbows and forearms were covered with blood and little pieces of gravel. "What happened?" the preacher inquired, hurrying to help his friend.

The man replied, "After I left you, I was on my way to town, and a big storm came up. I tried to outrun it, but the rain began to fall like lumps of lead. As I was going around the big curve, I hit some loose gravel and the motorcycle slid out from under me. I skidded more than 100 feet on the pavement. I managed to get up, but the motorcycle was a total loss. Somehow I staggered to a nearby farmhouse. As I walked up to the door, a frightened woman pointed a shotgun in my direction. I started running and she started shooting. I ran through the brush and briars and got all scratched up. Finally, I came into a clearing and found a tree to shield me from the rain. As I stood there picking the buckshot from my back, lightning struck the tree and knocked me out. I came to and in a daze simply started walking down the road."

The preacher asked, "Where are you going now?"

The man replied, "I am going home." And then he added, "If it be the Lord's will."

James 4:15 is calling us to get our priorities in order. Some of us have forsaken the priorities of God's will and God's way in our lives.

God's Will

God wants us to know His will and to walk in it. Paul said, "We have not stopped praying for you and asking God to fill you with the knowledge of his will through all spiritual wisdom and understanding" (Colossians 1:9). James also wanted to make sure that God is in our plans.

Waiting on God's will, however, is not a license for Christians to sit back and do nothing, or to live with no motivation or spirit of conquest. Some people are always waiting on the Lord's will. But there are times when we need to take the initiative. Jesus healed the man with the withered hand after he stretched out his hand. Christians ought to be the most motivated, positive-thinking, goal-oriented people in their communities because they are doing their work as unto the Lord.

Whatever our work, being in the will of God should characterize our lives. We should follow the example of the Apostle Paul. His desire was to be in the will of God. Before he left Ephesus, Paul said, "I will come back if it is God's will" (Acts 18:21). He wrote to the Corinthians, "I will come to you very soon, if the Lord is willing" (1 Corinthians 4:19). He wrote to the Romans, "I pray that now at last by God's will the way may be opened for me to come to you" (Romans 1:10). This incredible man was wise enough to know that all of his plans should have an addendum: "If it is the Lord's will."

Seeking God's will, Paul was led to Macedonia, "concluding" it was the will of God for his life (Acts 16:10). The Greek word translated "concluding," συμβιβάζω, means "it all came together." Συμβιβάζω suggests a picture of a sweater being knitted and finally coming together, or a jigsaw puzzle being completed. When we are in the will of God, the pieces of our lives will all come together. Being in the will of God is the secret to victory in the Christian life.

To avoid spiritual recession, we need to keep our priorities straight. We need to seek God's will as we make our plans. His desires should become our desires. Psalm 37:4 says, "Delight yourself in the Lord and he will give you the desires of your heart."

God's Way

Forsaken priorities involve God's way as well as God's will. James 4:17 says, "Anyone, then, who knows the good he ought to do and doesn't do it, sins." Translated "sins," the Greek word, ἁμαρτία, means "to miss the mark." The Greek writers used ἁμαρτία in three ways. In the physical dimension, it conveyed the picture of an archer who shoots the arrow toward the target and misses the bulls-eye. In the mental dimension, it conveyed the picture of a student who sits down to take a test and misses the answer. In the spiritual dimension, it conveyed the picture of a man who knows a certain standard is right but falls below it.

For the most part we only think of sins of commission — things we know we should not do, but do anyway. However, according to James, our real problem as believers is not in what we do, but in what we don't do — the sins of omission. Doing wrong is sin, but not doing right is just as sinful. For example, it is a sin to tell a lie, but it is also a sin to know the truth and not tell it.

Those who know what they ought to do and willfully refuse to do it are people with forsaken priorities. There is a sense in which they are worse than those with foolish presumptions. Second Peter 2:21 says, "It would have been better for them not to have known the way of righteousness, than to have known it and then to turn their backs on the sacred command that was passed on to them." Note carefully that James 4:17 is talking about the things we "know" we ought to do. One Greek word translated "know," οιδα, means "knowledge by reflection." Another Greek word also translated "know" means "to know by experience." James here used οιδα, implying that "we do not have to experience something to know whether it is right or wrong."[4] We know by reflection what we ought to do and what we ought not to do without having to experience the consequences.

What happens as a result of sins of commission? Do you remember when you sinned as a young person and felt so unclean? You came home afraid to face those who loved you most although they knew nothing about your sin. You were full of guilt. You lay down on your bed, turned the light off and tossed in anguish. But the next week when you went out and did the same thing, it bothered you but not quite as much. The more you continued committing that particular sin, the harder your heart became until you finally reached the place where that sin really didn't bother you anymore.

This sequence of events not only happens after sins of commission, but also after sins of omission. For instance, let's say a man sits in church and hears an invitation to come to Christ. He knows in his heart God is calling him. The conviction of God is upon him, but he leaves without making a decision. Oh, he comes back and again senses the call, but he again refuses. The time comes when his heart is so hardened to the gospel call through the sin of omission that he no longer hears the call, though he attends church every Sunday.

If you miss Heaven, it will not be because of sins of commission. It will be because of the sin of omission. Jesus says, "Whoever believes in him is not condemned, but whoever does not believe stands condemned already because he has not believed in the name of God's one and only Son" (John 3:18). The sin of not believing on the Lord Jesus Christ is a sin of omission.

If you are among those who think there will always be adequate time to get right with God, remember that you do not know when your heart is going to stop. "Today, if you hear his voice, do not harden your hearts" (Psalm 95:7–8). Take James' advice and do not make any foolish presumptions about tomorrow. And to avoid spiritual recession, maintain a proper perspective on life and keep your priorities in order. Guard against the arrogance of our age.

⊛ CHAPTER TEN ⊛

YOUR MONEY TALKS...
WHAT DOES IT SAY?
JAMES 5:1–6

I. How We Get It (James 5:1, 4, 6)
II. How We Guard It (James 5:1–3)
III. How We Give It (James 5:5)

"Now listen, you rich people..." With these five words, James begins the next paragraph of his letter. Many of us are prone to skip over this paragraph, erroneously feeling that it does not apply to us. We think this passage is for the men and women who live in the multi-million-dollar homes on the water. We may think, *Yes, Lord, give it to those rich snobs!*

There are basically two reactions to James 5:1–6. Some without money somehow feel that they are more spiritual than those who have money. Well, they are not. On the other hand, some who have money somehow feel as if they have to be defensive. Well, they don't. These verses apply to everyone, for being "rich" is relative. Compared to the rest of the world, almost everyone reading this book is filthy rich. Most of us have automobiles with power steering. We can afford to buy hamburgers for lunch. Most of the world's people cannot.

I wish I could take each of you out into the African bush a few miles from Mombasa, Kenya, in East Africa. I have preached in some churches there. It is not uncommon for 3,000 or 4,000 people to walk miles to attend the services. They sit on the ground, not on pews. If their pastor were to preach on James 5:1–6 this coming Sunday, they would be thinking about people in America who make the minimum wage when they heard the words,

"Now listen, you rich people..."

No matter how much we have, someone else has more. No matter how little we have, someone else has less. These words in James 5:1–6 are for each of us. I know many poor people who are more preoccupied with money and possessions than some wealthy people. The real issue is not whether we have money, but whether money has us. James was touching a sensitive nerve here regarding the danger of materialism — being possessed by things.

Many of us think that all we need to solve our problems is money. We think if we just had a little more money, we could take care of this or take care of that and then we would finally be happy. But what happens when money comes? The more money we have, the more we need. The more we make, the more we spend. We get a raise and usually it just helps us get a little more in debt. Money is deceptive. It can so subtly and unconsciously become our god. If we are not careful, it begins to possess us instead of our possessing it.

There is nothing wrong with wealth itself. Genesis 13:2 says, "Abram had become very wealthy in livestock and in silver and gold." First Chronicles 29:28 says that the psalmist David "died at a good old age, having enjoyed long life, wealth and honor." King Solomon, the writer of Proverbs, had more than Abraham and David put together. Joseph of Arimathaea, who furnished a tomb and arranged for our Lord to have a decent burial, had tremendous wealth (Matthew 27:57). Barnabas, a wealthy landowner, made possible the expansion of the early church by selling some valuable real estate on the island of Cyprus and giving the proceeds to the apostles. No wonder his name means "son of encouragement."

If there is nothing wrong with wealth, what was James saying? He was trying to tell us that the problem with wealth lies not in having it, but in how we get it, how we guard it and how we give it.

The way we deal with our money can bring "misery" upon us (James 5:1). The compound Greek word translated "misery," ταλαιπωρία comes from a word which means "to undergo or to endure,"[1] and a word which means "callous or that which brings joy only momentarily but is followed by misery." Getting our money by ungodly means will bring misery sooner or later. If we hoard our money, we will be of all men most miserable. And if we give our money to self-indulgence, the result will be misery. James warned of misery to come upon those who misuse their wealth, but he did not say that wealth in itself is wrong. We should not misunderstand what he was saying. His point was that how we get our money, how we guard it and how we give it reveals our true values to the whole world.

Our money talks. In fact, it says volumes about what we really think is important. It is so much a reflection of what is inside us that Jesus spoke often about it. One out of every three of His sermons had to do with money. Jesus told 38 parables, and one-third of them dealt with possessions. He said, "Where your treasure is, there your heart will be also" (Matthew 6:21). He was a diagnostician. And in a very real sense, the accountant who prepares our tax returns knows more about us spiritually than our Sunday school teachers or prayer partners. How we deal with our money is a reflection of our spiritual health.

I. How We Get It
James 5:1, 4, 6

The issue of how we get our wealth is so vitally important that the thought pervades the first paragraph of James 5. When writing this passage, James had in mind a man who received his money through exploitation and expropriation.

Exploitation

"Look! The wages you failed to pay the workmen who mowed your fields are crying out against you," James said. "The cries of the harvesters have reached the ears of the Lord Almighty" (James 5:4). The Bible never condemns the acquisition of wealth by legal and legitimate means. At issue here is the acquisition of wealth by illegal and illegitimate means. The man who received his wealth through exploitation had promised to pay his employees a certain amount, but when they completed their work, he refused to pay them. The phrase "failed to pay" is a translation of a Greek word, which refers to an illegitimate or fraudulent action.[2] From the very beginning, this man had no intention of paying his workers. He was always looking for loopholes in the contract to get out of paying what he owed. Because of this, he came under God's judgment.

Throughout the Old and New Testaments, God warns us not to acquire our wealth through exploitation. In Leviticus 19:13 we read, "Do not defraud your neighbor or rob him. Do not hold back the wages of a hired man overnight." Deuteronomy 24:14–15 tells us, "Do not take advantage of a hired man who is poor and needy, whether he is a brother Israelite or an alien living in one of your towns. Pay him his wages each day before sunset, because he is poor and is counting on it. Otherwise, he may cry to the Lord against you, and you will be guilty of sin." Exodus 2:23 tells us that God heard the cries of the slaves in Egypt: "The Israelites groaned in their slavery and cried out, and their cry for help because of their slavery went up to God." In Luke 10:7, Jesus says, "The worker deserves his wages."

The tense of the verbs in James 5:4 is important to the understanding of the verse. The verb translated "mowed" is aorist, indicating the task had been accomplished. The verb translated "failed to pay" is in the imperfect tense, indicating that the employer held back the wages permanently and had no intention of paying what was due. The verb translated "crying out against you" is in the present tense, indicating the continuous crying out of these wages.[3] The employees began to cry out to God about this injustice. We will see later that pay day comes sooner or later.

Remember the term "rich" is relative. We do not have to be employers to be guilty of exploitation. Some employees exploit their employers. For example, suppose your employer pays you for eight hours of work a day. You show up 10 or 15 minutes late, take an extra five minutes on your morning and afternoon breaks, come back from lunch 15 minutes late, sit at your desk and read a magazine or do your nails, and then leave a few minutes early. You have only put in about six and a half hours of work, not the eight you agreed to. You are just as guilty of exploitation as the man who did not pay a fair wage. If your employer pays you for an eight-hour day and you only work seven hours, you are stealing from him. You might as well go into the petty-cash box and take out the money.

Christians in the workforce ought to work harder than anyone else because they are doing their jobs unto the Lord (Ephesians 6:5–8). Ill-gotten gains will come back to haunt us. We must guard against acquiring our wealth through exploitation.

Expropriation

James made a stinging accusation: "You have condemned and murdered innocent men, who were not opposing you" (James 5:6). The man James had in mind not only gained his wealth through exploitation but also through expropriation. The Greek word translated "condemned," καταδικάζω, is a judicial term suggesting the manner in which the rich pervert the legal system to accumulate their wealth. The term speaks of those who control the courts in such a way that justice is eliminated. In other words, they have the power to use the courts to take away someone else's means of support. The man who exploited his workers had the political power to control the system and prevent his employees from opposing him. Thus he deprived them of their livelihood. It was just as if he had murdered them.[4]

There are ways of killing people without taking away their physical lives. We can kill a person's reputation through slander. We can kill a person's incentive through constant agitation. James was thinking of a man who stepped over anything or anyone he had to in order to reach the top.

The victims did not offer opposition because the system controlled by the rich rendered them unable to retaliate. James 2:6 says, "Is it not the rich who are exploiting you? Are they not the ones who are dragging you into court?" To exploit is bad enough, but it is worse still to expropriate when resistance is impossible. In the end, wealth gained by expropriation can only bring misery.

We cannot help but remember that the love of money was at the root of Christ's betrayal. Judas loved money. Yes, he received 30 pieces of silver and look how he got it. He is the epitome of someone who ended up weeping and wailing.

Yes, our money talks. What is it saying about how we got it? If we have obtained our wealth through exploitation or expropriation, our gold and silver will testify against us.

II. How We Guard It
James 5:1–3

How we guard our money is also revealing. The man James had in mind "hoarded" his wealth (James 5:3). "Hoarded" is a translation of the Greek word θησαυρίζω, from which we get our word "thesaurus." It means "a collection" and has the connotation of gathering all we can and storing it up. Now there is nothing wrong with a savings account. In fact, the Bible puts its stamp of approval on fiscal responsibility (see 2 Corinthians 12:14 for an example). But it is wrong to hoard wealth that is owed to others. James said that guarding such wealth is deceitful, decadent and deceptive.

Deceitful

Guarded wealth promises joy but only brings misery. When we begin to love money, it ceases to bless us and begins to curse us. We think that just a little more money will make us happy, but that is a deception.

The parable of the rich fool illustrates the deceitfulness of guarded wealth. Jesus said, "This is how it will be with anyone who stores up things for himself but is not rich toward God" (Luke 12:21). The man in the parable accumulated wealth "for himself" with utter disregard for anything or anyone else. So God said, "You fool! This very night your life will be demanded from you. Then who will get what you have prepared for yourself?" (12:20) We sometimes think a new suit, a new car or a new home will make us happy. But these things never really satisfy. They are all deceitful.

It is good to have things money can buy, but it is better to have the things money cannot buy. To illustrate, I have a small diamond stickpin that I used to wear on my ties. It has not always been a stickpin. When my wife, Susie, and I were married in 1970, the diamond in the stickpin was the diamond in her wedding ring. I was a student in those days and could only afford a wedding ring with that one small diamond. If you examine it closely, you will see a big carbon chip in the middle of it;

the jeweler sold it to me for slightly more than $100. However, symbolized in that ring was a tremendous amount of love and the knowledge that God had brought us together. About the same time, a college friend gave his fiancée one of the biggest, most beautiful diamond rings I have ever seen, worth multiplied thousands of dollars. Tragically, their marriage did not last a year.

Money can buy million-dollar houses, but all the money in the world cannot transform those houses into homes. Behind mahogany doors and iron gates are some of the most miserable people in the world. What is really important is not what money can buy, but what money cannot buy. Andrew Carnegie, who will always be remembered as one of America's greatest entrepreneurs, said:

> *I was born in poverty and would not exchange its sacred memories with the richest millionaire's son who ever breathed. What does he know about a mother or a father? These are mere names to him. Give me the life of the boy whose mother is nurse, seamstress, washer woman, cook, teacher, angel and saint all in one, and whose father is guide, exemplar, and friend. No servants to come between. These are the boys who are born to the best fortune. Some men think that poverty is a dreadful burden and that wealth leads to happiness. What do they know about it? They know only one side. They imagine the other. I have lived both, and I know there is very little in wealth that can add to human happiness beyond the small comforts of life. Millionaires who laugh are rare.[5]*

Yes, hoarded wealth is deceitful.

Decadent

Money can also be decadent. It decays. If we don't use it, we lose it. We cannot take it with us when we die. It is temporal. Only what we deposit in the bank of Heaven will last. That which is used for God's glory never fades away. Jesus says, "Do not store up for yourselves treasures on earth, where moth and rust destroy, and where thieves break in and steal. But store up for yourselves treasures in heaven, where moth and rust do not destroy, and where thieves do not break in and steal" (Matthew 6:19–20).

Emphasizing the perishable nature of worldly riches, James 5:2, 3 says, "Your wealth has rotted, and moths have eaten your clothes. Your gold and silver are corroded." All three verbs are in the perfect tense; James was so certain of the temporary nature of riches that he described their decay as having already happened. He was showing us the present worthless state of our possessions.[6]

The first-century world did not have certificates of deposit or stock certificates. Their wealth was measured in grain, garments and gold. When James said, "Your wealth has rotted," he was referring to grain. A man's worth was often determined by the amount of grain he could store in his barn. Remember the rich fool had many goods laid up for future years. But grain rots. How does grain rot? By lack of use. Our guarded wealth, like grain, is decadent. If we don't use it, it does us no good and we eventually lose it.

When James said, "Moths have eaten your clothes," he knew that in the ancient world, garments were also symbols of wealth. When Joseph blessed his brothers in Egypt, he gave them garments (Genesis 45:22). Lust for a Babylonian robe led to the downfall of Achan (Joshua 7:21). Naaman, commander-in-chief of the Syrian army, brought Elisha garments as a gift (2 Kings 5:5).

The man James had in mind made his money for the express purpose of showing off to others how rich he was; he wanted to be noticed by his fancy and flashy outer garments. (The Greek word translated "clothes" in James 5:2, ἱμάτιον, means "outer garment.") But garments ruin.[7] Moths eat them.

A moth is subtle and silent, lurking behind the scenes. He eats away at our treasures and before we know it, they are gone. A moth is not like other insects. A roach will badger and taunt us. He will eat away at our cabinets and leave his droppings on the drain board. A cricket will bug us (no pun intended) by making noise and remaining hidden. A mosquito will bite us. A fly will bother us. But a moth will beguile us. He keeps to himself. He will not badger, bug, bite or bother us. He will not gnaw at us or make a lot of noise. He'll simply hang out in the back of the closet and work in secret until it is too late.

Moths eat our clothes when they hang in our closets for long periods of time. Garments ruin because of lack of use. Likewise, when we guard our wealth instead of using it, it decays. We do not see our riches being eaten away, but before we know it, they are gone.

Grain rots, garments ruin and gold rusts. James 5:3 says, "Your gold and silver are corroded." Again, it is lack of use that causes decay. A hinge on a gate that hasn't been opened in a long time can become corroded. A pair of pliers left outside can gather so much rust that they can hardly be opened. The Greek verb translated "corroded," κατιόω, is singular, indicating that James was speaking of gold and silver as a symbolic unit. He was talking about assets that symbolize our wealth. The Greek preposition κατα (the first part of κατιόω) means "through," indicating that the gold and silver are completely corroded.[8] The point of the illustration is that unused wealth that is hoarded and guarded is decadent.

But most of us know that real gold will not rust. Therefore,

James was also saying that our wealth is actually fool's gold. It has no eternal value. What a disappointment to discover that what we thought was valuable is worthless. Guarded wealth is both deceitful and decadent.

Deceptive

Wealth brings a false sense of security. The stock market is up one day and down the next. Money markets and financial accounts fluctuate from hour to hour. Riches are uncertain. James' contemporaries experienced the deceptiveness of guarded wealth firsthand. Within a few years after James wrote his epistle, Jerusalem was destroyed by the Romans and the Jews' accumulated wealth was taken. This siege in A.D. 70 brought famine and disease. The situation was so bad that those who had been wealthy before, were now reduced to such demoralizing and depraved activities as cannibalism.

It is a mistake to think that security is found in wealth. It is also a mistake to think that it is good stewardship to guard our wealth. James 5:3 says our corroded gold and silver will testify against us. Wealth is deceptive. The man James had in mind guarded his wealth in self-defense, but in the final analysis, his wealth was used against him. How ironic. The question at the judgment seat of Christ is not going to be, "How much did you make?" The question will be, "What did you do with what you had?" Your money talks!

Hoarding our wealth affects not just ourselves, but others as well. James 5:3 says, "You have hoarded wealth in the last days." The last days began with Christ's ascension and will end with His second coming. We may be nearing the end of the last days. The question is, how will we use our wealth in these days of tremendous evangelistic opportunity? Too many of us guard wealth rather than give it to the Lord's work.

James reminded us that these guarded resources will testify against us and eat our flesh like fire. They will expose us. This is a serious warning, not an irrelevant addendum. James' words ought to make us sit up on the edge of our seats. There are many people who do not believe that ultimately they will be punished by God. They think of God only as a God of love. However, the same God who says that He is a God of love says that He is a God of justice.

God is as concerned with how we guard our wealth as He is with how we get it. What are we going to do with the money we have hoarded up anyway? One day each of us is going to die and someone else is going to spend it. In many cases, our money will only cause our heirs misery because it will take away their incentive to work. Our influence for good or bad will continue after we are gone. All the accounts are not in yet. This is why our judgment awaits Christ's return. We will not be judged as soon as we die.

As I pen these words, I am thinking about how fortunate I am. My family loves the Lord Jesus Christ, and they unashamedly stand up for Him. After more than 40 years of marriage, my wife and I have put a significant percentage of our money into the Lord's work, primarily through our local church fellowship and through Mission:Dignity, supporting our dear retired pastors and in most cases, their widows, who have deep financial needs. We invest in the bank of Heaven. That is why our hearts are in our church. I am going to leave my children something far more valuable than a pile of money to hoard and guard. I have sought to teach them the importance of laying up treasures in Heaven. I want them to know that our treasures do not follow our hearts; our hearts follow our treasures. If we wait until we feel like giving, we will never do it. Jesus says, "Where your treasure is, there your heart will be also" (Matthew 6:21).

It is a great tragedy to come to the end of life and have

treasure laid up in this world only. We came into this world without anything, and we will leave the same way. We do not own our possessions. They all belong to God, and we are but stewards. People who hoard the possessions they think they own will one day weep and wail in misery (James 5:1).

Their problem was not in possessing money, but in letting it possess them. Money is not the root of all evil. Paul said, "The *love* of money is a root of all kinds of evil" (1 Timothy 6:10, *italics added)*. Those who are deceived into loving money will covet. Although "You shall not covet" (Exodus 20:17) is the last of all the Ten Commandments, it may be the most dangerous command to break.[9] Covetousness makes a person break the other nine commandments. David broke the seventh commandment — "You shall not commit adultery" — because he broke the tenth and coveted Bathsheba. Gehazi broke the eighth commandment "You shall not steal" — because he broke the tenth and coveted Naaman's riches.

There is nothing wrong with money, but money that is guarded will never spread the gospel of Jesus Christ. However, money in the hands of a good steward can be a testimony. At the end of your life, will you be considered a hoarder or a steward? Your Last Will and Testament is your last testimony. It is read at the end of your life, and it says what is really important to you. What does your will say as a testimony of Jesus Christ? Yes, your money talks.

III. How We Give It
James 5:5

Our money talks primarily by how we give it. Some people simply give their money to themselves in self-indulgence, while others give it to the Lord to advance His kingdom. The man

James had in mind gave his ill-gotten gains to himself. He "lived on earth in luxury and self-indulgence" (James 5:5). The word for "luxury," τρυφάω, means "extravagant comfort,"[10] "to lead a soft life."[11] The word for "self-indulgence," σπαταλάω, means "to give oneself to pleasure."[12] Σπαταλάω is also found in 1 Timothy 5:6: "The widow who lives for pleasure is dead even while she lives." (See Jesus' parable of the rich man and Lazarus in Luke 16:19–31 for another example of someone who lived in luxury.)

James 5:5 continues, "You have fattened yourselves in the day of slaughter." This image communicates well to me because I grew up in Fort Worth, Texas, where the famous stockyards are found on the north side of town at the beginning of the old Chisholm Trail. If you were to walk the streets of the North Side today, you would see cattle penned up in the stockyards. They are given the finest of grain and do not realize that they are going to be slaughtered. Consequently, they eat and eat and eat, taking the pleasures of the moment. And the more they eat, the quicker they will be led to the slaughterhouse. When they are all fattened up, the workers throw a little corn in front of the stupid cows, and their desire for self-indulgence and luxury entices them right out of the pen and into the slaughterhouse next door.

James was saying that some of us are like those Texas steers. We just keep fattening ourselves, not knowing that we are hastening the day of our own slaughter. The slaughterhouse represents the judgment to come. Those who guard their wealth and give it only to themselves are blind to the fact that they are headed toward a day of reckoning. They follow their selfish appetites and are too blind to see that it is to the ruin of relationships or to the ruin of self-respect.

One day we will stand before our Creator. He is not going to say, "Let me see your Bible. Is it all marked up?" Nor is He going to say, "Let me see your sermon notebook. Are there any notes in it?" Nor will He say, "Let me see your prayer journal. Have you prayed every day and written it down?" Nor will He say, "Let me see your Sunday school record. Do you have perfect attendance?" Some of us are going to be shocked when we stand before God. I think He may say, "Let me see your checkbook. I want to see your cancelled checks." How we use our resources reveals what is really important to us. Our money talks.

There are some supernatural laws that should govern our giving. There is the law of clarification, which states that God owns all the wealth in this world and the next. In David's words, "Everything in heaven and earth is yours" (1 Chronicles 29:11). "The earth is the Lord's and everything in it" (Psalm 24:1).

The law of circulation states that God wants His wealth in circulation. In God's economy, the earth had one theme in the beginning: give, give, give. The sun gave. The earth gave. The animals gave. The man gave. The trees gave. But Satan came and introduced a new concept: get, get, get. Man became greedy and began to live by Satan's philosophy, but God's original design for the use of resources still applies.

The law of cooperation states that all of God's wealth belongs to His children. The problem is, they are not cooperating with Him. Paul said, "We are heirs — heirs of God, and co-heirs with Christ" (Romans 8:17).

Finally, the law of cultivation states that the way to appropriate God's wealth is to give. We never reap until we sow. Jesus says, "Give, and it will be given to you. A good measure, pressed down, shaken together and running over, will be poured into your lap. For with the measure you use, it will be measured to you" (Luke 6:38). To coin a phrase, we are to "give out of God's hand." We are to reach into His unlimited resources and give from Him to others. What a privilege. Perhaps King David said it best: "Everything comes from you, and we have given you only what comes from your hand" (1 Chronicles 29:14).

We live in a world where accumulation is the name of the game. Caught in this trap, many of us get everything we can and guard it as long as we can. Some of us foolishly think that the issue at the judgment bar of Christ will be: "How much have you accumulated?" or "How much have you guarded?" But let's not for a moment think that our Righteous Judge will look at us and ask, "How much did you make?" His question will be, "What kind of steward were you? What did you do with what I gave you?"

The fundamental danger inherent in having wealth lies in the fact that it can cause us to focus our complete attention on this world. We may begin to live for this world alone. Once we possess wealth, it may begin to possess us. The Christian must beware of the danger. He must get his wealth honestly, guard it loosely and give it selflessly to Christ.

As we have seen, it is not what we guard but what we give that makes us rich. When we guard earthly treasure, it rots, ruins and rusts. And one day it will stand up to testify against us. Yes, your money talks. Does it say, "Get me any way you can, whether it be through exploitation or expropriation"? Does it say, "Guard me, hold me tight, keep me, clutch me"? If so, you of all people are most miserable. Does your money say, "Spend me on yourself and no one else"? If so, it has become your master. Or does it say, "Give me away to others in the service of Jesus"? If so, you know the peace and joy that can only come from Jesus Christ.

⊛ CHAPTER ELEVEN ⊛

APOCALYPSE NOW?
JAMES 5:7–12

1. Look Up...Be Calm (James 5:7)
II. Look In...Be Clean (James 5:8–9)
III. Look Back...Be Challenged (James 5:10–11)
IV. Look Forward...Be Consistent (James 5:12)

"Be patient...until the Lord's coming" (James 5:7). As I read these words, I immediately think of all the prophets of doom who take every world event and try to fit it into Scripture, often causing panic and concern among the family of faith. These words cause me to flash back several decades to my grandmother's lap and a worn-out book about Chicken Little.

Chicken Little was scratching under a tree when an acorn fell and hit him on the tail. He began to shout, "Oh, the sky is falling; I am going to tell the king!" Along the way, he met a hen and shared the story. The hen decided to accompany Chicken Little, and along the way they met a rooster.

The hen told the rooster, "The sky is falling down." When the rooster inquired as to how the hen had heard this, the hen replied that Chicken Little had told her.

Chicken Little then said, "I saw it with my own eyes and heard it with my own ears, and a piece of it hit me." As the three journeyed to tell the king, they met a duck, a goose and a turkey, all of whom joined them.

Finally the group met a fox. When Chicken Little told the story of how he had seen it with his own eyes and heard it with his own ears, and a part of it had fallen and hit him, the sly fox said, "Let's go into my den, and I'll tell the king." The last line of the book simply says, "So they all ran into Foxy Loxy's den and the king was never told that the sky was falling!"

Today many people are crying, "This is it; the sky is falling!" In past years people have stockpiled freeze-dried foods and other supplies in preparation for Armageddon. Attention has been diverted from appropriating all the blessings of Christ's first coming by those who cry in panic, "The sky is falling!"

But the beautiful fact is that our Lord will return to this earth. It will be the greatest event in all of human history, and it could happen today! The same Jesus who came the first time as a suffering servant is coming again as the King of kings and the Lord of lords. As we think about the second coming of Christ, several questions immediately come to mind: What? Whose? Why? Where? and When?

What is the second coming? The Greek word translated "coming" in James 5:7 is παρουσία, which means "being with." In secular Greek, παρουσία was a technical expression for a royal visit of a king or one in authority. Paul used the word to indicate the physical presence of Titus when he said, "God, who comforts the downcast, comforted us by the coming of Titus" (2 Corinthians 7:6). Jesus used the same word when He said, "As it was in the days of Noah, so it will be at the coming of the Son of Man" (Matthew 24:37). Jesus Christ will come again, bodily. His presence will be with us. He will invade this world, conquer evil and usher in the original "new age." The return of Christ is what Paul called "the blessed hope" (Titus 2:13).

The next question is *"Whose?"* It is the Lord's παρουσία. In the upper room, He promised that He would return (John 14:3). The angel on the mount of Olives said, "This same Jesus, who has been taken from you into heaven, will come back in the same way you have seen him go into heaven" (Acts 1:11). Revelation 22:20 (the verse that contains the last promise in the Bible and the last prayer recorded in the Bible) says: "He who testifies to these things says, 'Yes, I am coming soon.' Amen. Come, Lord Jesus."

This brings us to the third question, "*Why* is He coming again?" He came the first time as a suffering servant. However, He will return the second time as the "Son of Righteousness with healing in His wings," the King of kings and Lord of lords. He will come in judgment to separate the wheat from the chaff. He will come to execute judgment. As James 5:9 says, "The Judge is standing at the door!" At His coming He will usher in a new age of peace, followed by eternity.

The fourth question is "*Where?*" Christ will come first "in the air." Paul said: "After that, we who are still alive and are left will be caught up together with them in the clouds to meet the Lord in the air. And so we will be with the Lord forever" (1 Thessalonians 4:17). Then He will come to earth. "On that day his feet will stand on the Mount of Olives, east of Jerusalem, and the Mount of Olives will be split in two from east to west, forming a great valley, with half of the mountain moving north and half moving south" (Zechariah 14:4).

A final question is "*When?*" There is a great deal of speculation today that Christ's coming is imminent. Perhaps He will come very soon. Perhaps not. We do not know. In fact, Jesus said, "No one knows about that day or hour, not even the angels in heaven, nor the Son, but only the Father" (Matthew 24:36). We should live each day as though Christ could return any moment since we do not know exactly when He will come. We should, as Jesus reminds us, watch and pray. The Bible admonishes us to watch for several major signs that will usher in the return of our Lord Jesus Christ.

Watch for a Polluted Pulpit

The Bible tells us that a sure sign of the return of Jesus Christ is a turning away from the truth of the gospel by preachers and teachers. Paul said: "Preach the Word; be prepared in season and out of season; correct, rebuke and encourage — with great patience and careful instruction. For the time will come when men will not put up with sound doctrine. Instead, to suit their own desires, they will gather around them a great number of teachers to say what their itching ears want to hear. They will turn their ears away from the truth and turn aside to myths" (2 Timothy 4:2–4).

We are living in a day when denominations are dying before our very eyes. In the words of Jude, many preachers have "taken the way of Cain" (Jude 11). They have set aside the blood atonement of Christ and substituted the very best their human hands can offer instead. A polluted pulpit is a sure sign of the soon return of our Lord.

Watch for a Particular Place

Before Christ returns, the Bible says that Israel will re-emerge as a major player on the world scene. God said to us through the prophet Amos: "I will bring back my exiled people Israel; they will rebuild the ruined cities and live in them. They will plant vineyards and drink their wine; they will make gardens and eat their fruit. I will plant Israel in their own land, never again to be uprooted from the land I have given them" (Amos 9:14–15).

Our generation has seen some amazing developments in that "particular place" in the Middle East. The stage is being set for the return of our Lord.

Watch for a Peculiar People

After the wilderness wanderings, Moses stood at the Jordan River and preached a prophetic sermon before the children of Israel entered Canaan. He said, "The Lord will scatter you among the peoples, and only a few of you will survive" (Deuteronomy 4:27). Later he said: "You will become...an object of scorn and ridicule to all the nations where the Lord will drive you...Among those nations you will find no...resting place" (Deuteronomy 28:37, 65). But Ezekiel talked about that day when God would "gather [His people] from all the countries and bring [them] back into [their] own land" (Ezekiel 36:24).

While there is debate as to whether the present secular Zionist nation of Israel is indeed Biblical Israel, the fact remains that unusual things are happening among this "peculiar people." Although they are back in their land, they desperately need to heed the warning of the Torah in their relationship with the Palestinians. God said: "Do not mistreat an alien or oppress him, for you were aliens in Egypt" (Exodus 22:21).

Watch for a Powerful Politic

The Bible tells us that before Christ returns a powerful coalition of nations will emerge out of Europe. Daniel referred to them as the ten horns of the ancient Roman empire *(Daniel 7:15–25)*. These nations will become a vast economic and industrial power and form an alliance with every major world empire. They will eventually usher in a one-world government. We have seen this "new world order" emerge before our very eyes as Europe has moved toward a common currency and united politically.

Watch for a Popular Politician

The Bible reveals that shortly before the return of Christ, an electrifying leader will emerge on the world scene. The Bible calls him the Antichrist. First John 2:18 says: "Dear children, this is the last hour; and as you have heard that the antichrist is coming, even now many antichrists have come. This is how we know it is the last hour." This leader will promise to bring about a world order of peace. He will promise to free the world of war and provide solutions to the world's economic and political problems. Most of the world will follow him. Some believe this popular politician could even be alive at the present time.

Watch for a Pluralistic Philosophy

The Bible records that before Christ returns, a new religion will unite the world under one banner. A new age of humanistic thought will exalt man above Christ. Every time I see a crystal hanging from a rearview mirror on the automobile of a New Age follower, I join John the apostle in praying, "Come, Lord Jesus" (Revelation 22:20). This pluralistic philosophy that is sweeping the world is a sign of the times.

Instead of being patient while watching for these signs, many are presumptuous. There have always been those who try to forecast or pinpoint the Lord's parousia. Every major world event brings a new wave of preachers crying, "The sky is falling." This is one reason why preachers lose so much credibility.

The Balfour agreement in 1917, which officially ushered in the return of the Jews to Palestine during World War I, caused many preachers to shout, "The sky is falling." As we read prophetic books written during those days, we realize that the authors were sure that Christ's coming was imminent.

During World War II, preachers all over America were declaring that Hitler was the Antichrist. Panic set in among various people, and all the while the Bible continued to say, "Be patient... until the Lord's coming" (James 5:7).

Then came the aftermath of World War II and the United Nations' vote in May 1948 that startled the world by making Israel a nation again. Seeing that event, one prominent author took Jesus' words out of context and said, "This generation shall not pass until all these things be fulfilled." He said that a Biblical generation was 40 years and, therefore, Jesus Christ would return by 1988. Many preachers proclaimed this fact during the 1950s, 1960s, 1970s and 1980s — until 1989! I haven't heard it anymore. But all during those 40 years, they were crying, "The sky is falling."

Then came 1967 and the famous Six-Day War in Israel. For the first time since the days of Nebuchadnezzar, the Jews controlled Jerusalem. They returned to Israel in increasing numbers, and once again preachers began to cry, "The sky is falling. Jesus is coming." In 1982 when Israel began fighting with Lebanon, preachers began to pull out obscure Scriptural passages and tried to relate that crisis to the any-minute return of Christ. Again they cried, "The sky is falling."

Later in the 1980s, Soviet president Gorbachev and the mark on his forehead became the subject of speculation that he was the antichrist as he became prominent in the march for world peace. Other preachers were even subtly saying that George H.W. Bush could possibly be the Antichrist since he was seeking to make peace in the Middle East and was calling for a new world order.

In 1991, the Persian Gulf War erupted. It was strange how preachers and teachers who had interpreted Jeremiah 50–51 and Revelation 17–18 as the harlot of the world system suddenly saw Babylon in those chapters as modern-day Iraq. They conveniently reinterpreted the Bible to fit the current crisis and once again we heard the cry, "The sky is falling." And on and on we could go up until this present moment if space permitted it.

In our day, many are convinced that the present return of the Jews to Israel is the promised regathering. Personally, I am not convinced for several reasons. One, it is only a partial return and the Scripture says that every Jew will be gathered there one day (Ezekiel 36:10; 39:28; Isaiah 49:18). Two, the present return is gradual, and the Scripture says it will be in days, not in decades (Isaiah 11:1–12). Three, the present Jews who return are mostly unbelievers and much of the Israeli government is at best agnostic, secular and Zionist. This is in sharp contrast to the returning holy people mentioned in Isaiah 62:11–12 and Zephaniah 3:9–10. Scripture also says that God will gather His people after repentance (Isaiah 60:4–9) and that Israel will be spiritually reborn in a day (Isaiah 66:8).

The parousia — the Lord's coming — is our blessed hope and we can look expectantly to that great day, but we must not run after every pseudo prophet who cries, "The sky is falling." Christ may come today, next year, next century or next millennium. Only the Father knows (Mark 13:32).

The early believers lived with the conviction that Christ's coming was near. They fully believed it could happen any minute. They lived as though each day might be their last opportunity. We should live as though Christ died yesterday and the cross has not been taken down from Golgotha. We should live as though Christ arose today and the grave clothes are still lying in place. We should also live as though He will return tomorrow. We should live with the same expectancy as the early believers and yet "be patient until the Lord's παρουσία."

James 5:7–12 deals with what we are to do until the Lord's coming. We should look up and be calm, look in and be clean, look back and be challenged, and look forward and be consistent.

I. Look Up...Be Calm
James 5:7

Predictions of Christ's return are nothing new. They were occurring 30 years after the resurrection. So James admonished his first readers, "Be patient" (James 5:7). The Greek word translated "patient," μακροθυμεω, means "to be long-tempered, longsuffering, to have a long fuse." The word conjures up a picture of a distance runner who thinks of the long term as he runs and focuses on the final lap. James was saying, "Don't let momentary stumbles beset you. Look up and be calm."

Some of these first-generation believers to whom James wrote had become so anxious and eager for Christ's return that they were growing impatient. Some were beginning to crack under the pressure of persecution. So when James used the word "patient," he was calling on those Christians to "face even the most adverse circumstances with courage and calm."[1]

James encouraged this calmness "until" the Lord's parousia (James 5:7). Associated with this word "until" is the idea of waiting for, looking for or anticipating. A woman who has borne a child knows this experientially. A pregnant woman is full of anticipation, but the only thing she can do is be patient.

For two and a half years when I was a pastor in Hobart, Oklahoma, I ate breakfast every morning with a bunch of farmers at the A & B Cafe near the town square. I learned many Scriptural truths by listening to those farmers talk about their profession. Historians tell us that James was a farmer. Therefore, it is not surprising that he likened our patience in waiting for the Lord's coming to that of a farmer waiting for the harvest. He said, "See how the farmer waits for the land to yield its valuable crop and how patient he is for the autumn and spring rains" (James 5:7).

Farmers throughout the world must wait and be patient. In Palestine, for instance, they plow and sow in the autumn. Therefore, the autumn rains are necessary to soften the soil and to help the seeds germinate. The harvest is in the spring. A farmer counts on spring showers to help the crops mature. The farmer cannot bring about the autumn and spring rains. He is totally dependent upon the Lord. Therefore, the farmer waits patiently. The harvest is worth the wait. In the autumn, he looks up and is calm as he awaits the autumn rains. The same is true in the spring.

There is a period after the seeds are planted when there is no visible evidence that anything is growing, though God is at work underground. The farmer knows he cannot hurry his crop to harvest. He continues to wait patiently. This does not mean he takes off a few months and does nothing while hoping everything will be all right in the end. No, there is cultivating and watering to be done in the meantime. It should be the same with us. We cannot hurry Christ's return, but while we wait, we can work. Only God can bring the harvest, but while we await His return, we should plant the seed, cultivate the ground and work faithfully in anticipation of the harvest.

Waiting periods are never without trials and testings. Sometimes the weather stays too cold or too hot. If there is too much rain, the crop will rot. If there is too little rain, the crop will scorch. If there is too much hail, the crop will be stripped. If the freeze comes early, the crop will die. So what does a farmer do? He stays calm and patiently awaits the harvest.

James was telling us that we should await the Lord's coming like the farmer awaits the harvest, looking up and remaining calm. The farmer cannot control the weather, and we cannot tell our Lord when to return. During the waiting period, there will often be times of trials and testings. There will always be people wringing their hands and causing panic because of their fear of a coming world holocaust. There will always be people taking our attention off the blessings of Christ's first coming. But we should learn from the farmer. "Be patient until the Lord's coming."

II. Look In...Be Clean
James 5:8–9

When we are in a waiting period, it is easy to become irritated and frustrated. Some of us turn to holding grudges, murmuring and grumbling. There is also potential within us to become bitter and resentful toward others. During times like these, we should "stand firm" (James 5:8).

The Greek word translated "stand firm," στηρίζω, is in the active voice and means "to prop,"[2] "to strengthen your being." The subject is to take action. All too often, we want God or someone else to prop us up, but we must stand firm ourselves. Στηρίζω is used in Luke 9:51: "As the time approached for him to be taken up to heaven, Jesus *resolutely set out* for Jerusalem" *(italics added)*. Jesus knew what was ahead. He knew the pressure was building. He knew about the trials, the beatings and the cross. Yet He was patient and stood firm. Until the Lord returns, we should not only look up and be calm, but we should also stand firm against anything sinful in our hearts — that is, we should look in and be clean.

James 5:9 says, "Don't grumble against each other." The Greek verb translated "grumble," στενάζω, denotes a feeling that is internal and unexpressed.[3] It refers to that which is harbored within. So James was saying, "Look inside and be clean." He added, "The Judge is at the door!" The Greek word for "door" is plural here, so most commentators indicate that James was speaking of the doors to all believers' hearts. Jesus used this same imagery: "Here I am! I stand at the door and knock.

If anyone hears my voice and opens the door, I will come in and eat with him, and he with me" (Revelation 3:20). Jesus does not stand at the doors of our lips, but at the doors of our hearts. We may fool others with our hypocrisy, but not the Righteous Judge who stands at the door. Since the Lord's return is imminent, we cannot afford to hold grudges or harbor sin in our lives. The Judge knows what is in our hearts.

Nearly 2,000 years have passed since James penned these words, and the Judge at the door has not stepped through the threshold yet. However, we must remember that God is not on central standard time. In fact, He said that 1,000 years on His calendar are as but a day. Until the Lord returns, we must stay calm and stand firm against sin.

III. Look Back...Be Challenged
James 5:10–11

James called on us to look up, look in and look back to those who have gone before us. Their example should be a challenge. Aware that often in waiting periods we are tempted to give up, James said to take the prophets as examples of patience (James 5:10). They too were looking for the Lord. What persecution and suffering they endured as they awaited His coming! Jesus said, "O Jerusalem, Jerusalem, you who kill the prophets and stone those sent to you, how often I have longed to gather your children together, as a hen gathers her chicks under her wings, but you were not willing" (Matthew 23:37). Just before he was killed, Stephen reminded the Sanhedrin: "Was there ever a prophet your fathers did not persecute? They even killed those who predicted the coming of the Righteous One. And now you have betrayed and murdered him" (Acts 7:52).

We are challenged when we realize what has gone before us.

When I was young (those were the days when families ate every evening meal together), my mother cooked with an old cast-iron skillet. She was given new Teflon cookware, but she went back to that old skillet. She used it for decades. Things just seemed to taste better because that old skillet had years of "buildup" in it. Buildup, that which has gone before, is important.

I once attended a graduation ceremony at West Point on the Hudson River. The history and tradition — the buildup — at that military academy is atmospheric. Likewise, when you walk the halls of such institutions as Harvard or Yale, you can sense the buildup of academic tradition.

Anyone who ever walked out into center field at the old Yankee Stadium in New York and saw the monuments of such greats as Babe Ruth, Lou Gehrig and others who have gone before, knows how important tradition and buildup are in athletics. Those who play in the Yankee pinstripes are expected to perform better than members of other teams.

History and tradition are also important to the Christian life. That's why James reminded us to look back and be challenged as we await the parousia. Look back at Hosea. His marriage failed, but he hung in there. Look back at Daniel. He was thrown into the lion's den for standing firm, but God delivered him. Look back at Jeremiah. He was arrested as a traitor and thrown into an abandoned well to die, but he looked up and was calm, and God delivered him.

Hebrews 11 gives us a roll call of persecuted prophets. Those of us whose family members seek to pull us down should look back to Abel (Hebrews 11:4). Those of us who face misunderstandings should look back to Noah (11:7). Those of us who face a crisis of faith should look back to Abraham (11:8–10). Those of us who are up against the impossible should also look to Abraham (11:11). Those of us who have been used and abused should look back to

Joseph (11:22). Those of us who face a great task should look back to Moses (11:24–29). Those of us who face obstacles and walls that cannot be scaled or tunneled under should look back to Joshua (11:30). Those of us who face sins of the past should look back to Rahab (11:31). James was saying, "Look back and be challenged."

Hebrews 11:36–40 speaks of the patience of those who have gone before us: "Some faced jeers and flogging, while still others were chained and put in prison. They were stoned; they were sawed in two; they were put to death by the sword. They went about in sheepskins and goatskins, destitute, persecuted and mistreated — the world was not worthy of them. They wandered in deserts and mountains, and in caves and holes in the ground. These were all commended for their faith, yet none of them received what had been promised. God had planned something better for us so that only together with us would they be made perfect."

Having used the prophets as examples of patience in suffering, James reminded us of the perseverance of Job (James 5:11). The book of Job is divisible into three parts. The first section *(chapters 1–3)* records his *distress* when he lost his health, wealth and family. The next section *(chapters 4–31)* records his *defense* when he answered false accusations and debated his three friends. The final section *(chapters 38–43)* records his *deliverance* and how God honored Job and restored to him twice what he had before.

Everything was against Job. His health and wealth were gone, his friends turned on him and his own wife said, "Why don't you just curse God and die?" For a while it even seemed as though God was against him. Yet Job persevered. He could say: "Naked I came from my mother's womb, and naked I will depart. The Lord gave and the Lord has taken away; may the name of the Lord be praised... Though he slay me, yet will I hope in him; I will surely defend my ways to his face... I know that my

Redeemer lives, and that in the end he will stand upon the earth... But he knows the way that I take; when he has tested me, I will come forth as gold" (Job 1:21; 13:15; 19:25; 23:10). No wonder James called on us to look back to Job when we are tempted to give up.

All the admonitions to waiting Christians point back to the first two words of James 5:7: "Be patient." Impatience causes so many failures. Look back to Peter who almost committed murder in the garden of Gethsemane. Look back to Moses. Because he struck the rock in impatience, he was not permitted to enter the promised land. Look back to Abraham whose impatience, shown in not waiting for God's promise to be fulfilled, led to the birth of Ishmael. We should learn from their mistakes. Paul said, "For everything that was written in the past was written to teach us, so that through endurance and the encouragement of the Scriptures we might have hope" (Romans 15:4).

We are involved in the race of life. We are not at the start of the race, nor are we at the finish; we seem to be in the middle. Anyone who has ever run a relay race knows that the start is filled with enthusiasm. There is a new beginning and the excitement of the starter's gun. The finish has the thrill of reaching the goal, and that is what carries us down the backstretch. There is joy in breaking the tape. But the middle — when we are a long way from the start and the finish line still can't be seen — tests us. Here we are...awaiting the Lord's parousia. Many Christians have run before us and passed the baton from generation to generation. What are we to do? We are to look up and be calm, look in and be clean, and look back and be challenged.

IV. Look Forward...Be Consistent
James 5:12

We are also to look forward and be consistent. Our lives should match our lips and our walk should match our talk. James 5:12 says, "Do not swear." James was not talking about profanity here, but about oaths. In the first-century world, people rarely signed contracts as they do today. They swore oaths instead.

Oaths were an important part of Jewish life. God even used an oath. Hebrews 6:13–14, 17 says: "When God made his promise to Abraham, since there was no one greater for him to swear by, he swore by himself, saying, 'I will surely bless you and give you many descendants.'...Because God wanted to make the unchanging nature of his purpose very clear to the heirs of what was promised, he confirmed it with an oath." Matthew 26:63–64 provides another example of the use of the oath at the house of Caiaphas: "Jesus remained silent. The high priest said unto him, 'I charge you under oath by the living God: Tell us if you are the Christ, the Son of God.' 'Yes, it is as you say,' Jesus replied." The apostle Paul used an oath when he said, "I call God as my witness that it was in order to spare you that I did not return to Corinth" (2 Corinthians 1:23).

Why then does James 5:12 say, "Above all, my brothers, do not swear — not by heaven or by earth or by anything else"? The reason is that oaths had acquired a shady reputation. They were used so frequently that they had lost their significance. There were binding oaths and non-binding oaths, and loopholes abounded. People used oaths the way a child says, "I cross my heart and hope to die" while his fingers are crossed behind his back. Jesus condemned such perversion of the oath (Matthew 23:16–22).

James 5:12 reminds us of one of the instructions our Lord gave on a grassy hillside in Galilee. Jesus said: "Do not swear at all: either by heaven, for it is God's throne; or by the earth, for it is his footstool; or by Jerusalem, for it is the city of the Great King. And do not swear by your head, for you cannot make even one hair white or black. Simply let your 'Yes' be 'Yes,' and your 'No,' 'No'; anything beyond this comes from the evil one" (Matthew 5:34–37). It is dangerous to call on God to give witness to our lies and exaggerations. Jesus was saying in effect, "Say what you mean and mean what you say." We are to be consistent while we look forward to the parousia. What we profess on Sunday, we must practice on Monday. If we have said yes to Jesus Christ, then we must live as Christians should. Paul said, "Just as you received Christ Jesus as Lord, continue to live in him" (Colossians 2:6).

James was not forbidding the taking of oaths in a court of law, for example. Because we live in a world that is far from perfect, such oaths are necessary in a secular setting to guard against perjury and to make sure that the truth is spoken. It is a concession we must make. However, in the church such oaths ought to be unnecessary. When someone says, "Yes, I will follow Christ," he ought to do so. James' point was that we Christians ought to mean what we say. We ought to be men and women of integrity. Our words should be consistent with our actions.

James warned that if our lives are inconsistent, we will be "condemned" (James 5:12). To be condemned is to be judged. Each of us will one day give an account to Jesus as to whether our yes was yes and our no was no. The return of our Lord, who is "at the door" (5:9), should motivate us to look forward and be consistent in life and lip, and in walk and talk. Remember, the theme of the book of James is not faith and works, but faith that works. We see that theme emphasized again in James 5:12.

Instead of running around with a "Chicken Little" philosophy screaming, "The sky is falling," we should be patient until the

Lord's coming. We know about His spiritual presence and what a comfort it is to have Christ within us. But just as the disciples in James' day were living to see Christ again — to hug Him, to touch Him, to speak to Him — we also long to touch the hem of His garment, to experience His physical presence. We are thankful for His spiritual presence, but desire to see Him face to face.

Many world events point to what could possibly signal the soon return of our Lord. Yes, we are to watch for a polluted pulpit, a particular place, a peculiar people, a powerful politic, a popular politician and a pluralistic philosophy. When we see these things coming to pass, we are to look up, look in, look back and look forward. But the bottom line is to be patient.

There is a sense in which the parousia is not something that we can get ready for; it will come like lightning. Jesus said, "As lightning that comes from the east is visible even in the west, so will be the coming of the Son of Man" (Matthew 24:27). Paul said His coming will be like a "thief in the night" (1 Thessalonians 5:2). We cannot get ready; we must *be* ready.

Has the thought occurred to you that our Lord Jesus could return to rapture His church before you complete this chapter? Luke 12:40 says, "The Son of Man will come at an hour when you do not expect him." Whether the Lord comes soon or tarries, you can take James' advice and be calm, be clean, be challenged and be consistent while you wait.

....

⊛ CHAPTER TWELVE ⊛

....

THE CHURCH IN TOUCH WITH A HURTING WORLD
JAMES 5:13-18

I. The Situation (James 5:13-15)
II. The Solution (James 5:16)
III. The Secret (James 5:16-18)

Amazingly, James' letter is as relevant today as it was in the first century. He addressed all the major issues the church now faces. James 5:13–18 calls on the church to be in touch with a hurting world, and we live in a world of hurts. Hearts are hurting. Homes are hurting. Hopes are hurting. The tragedy of our day is that when most secular people hear the word "church," they think of a musty-smelling, irrelevant institution that is totally out of touch with this hurt, and out of touch with real human need.

Blame lies at the doorstep of the church, for too many churches have brought the world's values into the church instead of taking the church into the world. How does the church lose touch? People begin to doubt the Word of God and evolve into believing a universal philosophy that says everyone is eventually going to Heaven. Consequently, those people feel no urgency to share Christ in the marketplace. We often talk about religion and politics and all the other issues of life in the marketplace, but seldom about how a personal relationship with Jesus Christ can give one hope, purpose and peace. Since the church does not go into the world, the secular world infiltrates the church.

If you had told me when the Lord called me into the ministry in 1968 that I would see major evangelical denominations in America voting to delete songs mentioning the blood of Christ from their hymnals, I would have said that you had lost your mind. If you had told me that in my lifetime several major mainline denominations in America would advocate homosexual marriage and ordination of homosexual clergy as well as give its stamp of approval to sexual activity among mature teenagers, I would have told you that you had lost your mind. A major denomination task force's report on human sexuality stated: "In the past we have viewed marriage as a prerequisite to sexual intercourse and considered sex outside of marriage as sin. Those beliefs must change or the church will be seen increasingly as irrelevant to most people's lifestyles."

Do you see what is at stake? This report is saying that the church must conform to the lifestyles of the people. In other words, the task force seems to believe that the Bible is archaic and out of date and what really matters are the trends of secular, cultural society, not the authoritative pattern of Biblical living that people have been following for centuries.

The church must go into the world with the message of hope. We must not simply allow the world to infiltrate our domain and undermine our long-cherished Scriptural convictions. The church must be in touch with a hurting world. In addressing this issue, James dealt with the situation, the solution and the secret.

1. The Situation
James 5:13–15

Life is filled with pressure and pleasure. There are mountaintops and valleys, sunshine and rain, happiness and heartache. Whatever our situation, God enables us to cope with the task at hand. James 5:13–15 mentions three types of situations people may find themselves in. Some people are in pressure situations. Others are experiencing pleasure. Finally, there are people in pain.

People with Pressure

James 5:13 says, "Is any one of you in trouble? He should pray." The Greek word κακοπαθέω, translated "in trouble," means "to suffer the evil blows from the outside world."[1] James was talking to anyone who is under pressure. Physical, emotional or spiritual problems can cause the kind of pressure that seeks to take away our happiness. Generally, people under pressure are not happy.

James not only observed the unhappy condition of people with pressure; he also offered some counsel. He advised that when we are in trouble, we should pray. Why is prayer often our last resort? We do all we can do and then we say, "There's nothing left to do but pray." The first thing we ought to do when we are in trouble is pray.

During my years of pastoring, I saw many people in trouble. I saw some blame others and some blame God. I saw some go to pieces emotionally and others fall apart physically. I saw some pray, coming to God with their heartaches and receiving His peace that comes in the midst of the storms of life.

God said, "Call upon me in the day of trouble; I will deliver you, and you will honor me" (Psalm 50:15). First Peter 3:12 puts it like this: "For the eyes of the Lord are on the righteous and his ears are attentive to their prayer, but the face of the Lord is against those who do evil." And Joseph M. Scriven put the lesson of James 5:13 into his hymn "What a Friend We Have in Jesus":

> *Have we trials and temptations?*
> *Is there trouble anywhere?*
> *We should never be discouraged,*
> *Take it to the Lord in prayer.*
> *Can we find a friend so faithful*

Who will all our sorrows share?
Jesus knows our every weakness,
Take it to the Lord in prayer.

What should people with pressure do? Pray!

People with Pleasure

James 5:13 continues, "Is anyone happy? Let him sing songs of praise." The Christian life should be characterized by happiness and joy. The Greek word for "happy," εὐθυμέω, refers to the "well-being of the soul." A Christian is not happy because of what is going on in the outside world, but because of what is going on inside him. True happiness is found in God. Paul said, "For the kingdom of God is not a matter of eating and drinking, but of righteousness, peace and joy in the Holy Spirit" (Romans 14:17).

Having observed people with pleasure, James counseled them to sing songs of praise. The Greek word for "sing songs," ψάλλω, means "to pluck a stringed instrument with the hand, to play an instrument like a harp." This verb is used only four times in the New Testament. In Ephesians 5:19, it is translated "making melody" in the KJV and "make music" in the NIV. The early church was a praying and praising church. They prayed when they were hurting, and they praised when they were happy. They prayed when they had pressure, and they praised when they had pleasure.

Psalm 50:23 talks about people with pressure and people with pleasure: "He who sacrifices thank offerings honors me, and he prepares the way so that I may show him the salvation of God." Prayer and praise go hand in hand. They are both essential in meeting needs. It is ironic that in the average church one of the greatest weaknesses is a lack of vitality in prayer and praise.

People with Pain

James 5:14–15 is the only directive in Scripture concerning praying for the sick. Numerous passages record healing ministries, but here we receive instructions on how to pray for the sick. Interestingly, much of what we see in healing ministries today is directly opposed to James' teaching. Perhaps few verses in the entire Bible are as misunderstood, misapplied and misinterpreted as these.

James described a local church ministry at a member's bedside. After all, who is most in need of healing? Is it the person who can drive to the tent or the city auditorium where the healing meeting is taking place? Is it the one who has aches, pains and headaches? Or is it the one who cannot get out of bed or who is in the hospital? Most modern faith healers rent large auditoriums and invite people to come to them. However, those who are most in need can't get there.

Note James' directive: "Is any one of you sick? He should call the elders of the church to pray over him and anoint him with oil in the name of the Lord. And the prayer offered in faith will make the sick person well; the Lord will raise him up. If he has sinned, he will be forgiven" (James 5:14–15). James was not speaking here about a combination of psychotherapy and an eastern mind-over-matter technique. He was talking about the church being in touch with a hurting world.

There are many different interpretations of this passage. Some say that physical healing is always just a prayer away. Some say the call is to combine prayer and modern medicine. Still others have different ideas. Our task is to put aside our preconceived ideas and simply see what the Bible actually says. We will note the probe, the proposal, the procedure, the prayer and the provision.

The Probe

"Is any one of you sick?" (James 5:14) Was James speaking of physical sickness, or emotional sickness or even spiritual sickness? The key is in understanding the word "sick." It is a translation of the Greek word ἀσθενέω that literally means "without strength, to be weak." It can mean weakness in body, weakness in soul or weakness in spirit. Ασθενέω is translated "weak" in Romans 14:1–2: "Accept him whose faith is weak... One man's faith allows him to eat everything, but another man, whose faith is weak, eats only vegetables." The word also appears in Acts 20:35: "In everything I did, I showed you that by this kind of hard work we must help the weak."

Ironically, James used a different word for "sick" in verse 15 than he did in verse 14: "The prayer offered in faith will make the sick person well." The Greek word here, κάμνω, means "to be weary" and suggests weariness in mind.[2] This particular word appears only two other times in the entire New Testament. In Hebrews 12:3 it is translated "grow weary": "Consider him who endured such opposition from sinful men, so that you will not grow weary and lose heart." The other time the word appears is in Revelation 2:3: "You have persevered and have endured hardships for my name, and have not *grown weary*" *(italics added)*.

Evidently, James was thinking about someone who had grown weary in the struggles of life. James was writing to a church scattered because of persecution. These people were facing hostilities. They were experiencing troubles and trials. They were tempted to give out, to give in and to give up. They had grown weak and weary. James was not thinking about someone who had the flu or a headache.

Although James 5:14–15 can certainly be applied to the physically sick, James was writing primarily to those who are about to crack under the pressures and oppressions of life, those who are weak spiritually and morally and those who have grown weary.

Certainly, God is the great physician and can do anything, including physical healing. But in a sense, this passage has little to do with physical healing. It has to do with men and women who are weak and weary, discouraged and depressed, worried and wounded. James was asking in effect, "Is anyone among you weak and weary and does not have strength to pray?" The people in James 5:13 could pray, but those in James 5:15 had given out and given up. They needed help.

If the probe reveals that we are weary in the work, should we drop out or gird up? James proposed a solution.

The Proposal

James proposed that when we grow weary in the Lord's work, we should "call the elders of the church" (James 5:14). The Greek word for "call," προσκαλέω, means "to call alongside, to summon."[3] The "elders" (πρεσβύτεροι) are the men called and equipped by the Holy Spirit to serve the church as its spiritual leaders. Why should we call the elders? People who are weak spiritually and emotionally need someone upon whom to lean. They need someone from whom to draw strength.

The initiative is to be taken by those who are sick. We are not to complain that no one ever comes to visit us when we are sick. We are to take the initiative and call for the elders. In response to this initiative, the elders were instructed to perform a ministry of encouragement. Paul said, "We urge you, brothers, warn those who are idle, encourage the timid, help the weak, be patient with everyone" (1 Thessalonians 5:14).

The Procedure

When a sick person calls for the elders, they are to "pray over him and anoint him with oil" (James 5:14). (This procedure is a primary task of pastoral ministry. Acts 6:4 explains that deacons are appointed so that elders can give their attention to prayer and the ministry of the Word.)

In the Greek New Testament, two distinct words are translated "anoint." One of these words, ἀλείφω, means "to rub with oil." It is an outward anointing of the body.[4] This word is found in the story of the good Samaritan. "He went to him and bandaged his wounds, pouring on oil and wine. Then he put the man on his own donkey, took him to an inn and took care of him" (Luke 10:34). The wine was to fight infection and the oil was to soothe the hurt. The same Greek word is also found in Matthew 6:17: "When you fast, put oil on your head and wash your face." The same word is used in John 12:3: "Mary took about a pint of pure nard, an expensive perfume; she poured it on Jesus' feet and wiped his feet with her hair." The anointing has no religious significance in any of these cases.

The other word translated "anoint" is χριω. It occurs five times in the Greek New Testament. Χριω is a ceremonial anointing, always used in a sacred and symbolic sense. This word is used to describe the anointing of kings and is a symbol of the Holy Spirit. For example, it is found in Luke 4:18: "The Spirit of the Lord is on me, because he has anointed me to preach good news to the poor." Χριω is also found in Acts 4:27: "Indeed Herod and Pontius Pilate met together with the Gentiles and the people of Israel in this city to conspire against your holy servant Jesus, whom you anointed." Paul used the word in 2 Corinthians 1:21: "It is God who makes both us and you stand firm in Christ. He anointed us."

James 5:15 uses ἀλείφω, the secular word mentioned in the

parable of the good Samaritan. Literally, James was saying, "Let them oil him with oil," in the same way that the good Samaritan poured oil over the wounded man. Thus, James was not speaking about some ritual or ceremonial anointing to symbolize the Holy Spirit's power. The elders were not to dip the tips of their fingers in oil and put a drop on the sick person's forehead as a symbol of the Holy Spirit. Rather, they were to rub the sick person with oil in order to provide comfort. Their actions were to be practical, not symbolic.

A. T. Robertson, the brilliant New Testament scholar and professor of a past generation, pointed out that olive oil was one of the best medicinal commodities of first-century Palestine. Even today, people in Palestine "swear by it" for both external and internal use — for stomach ailments and as a body oil.

In this admonition, James was saying that sick people should be treated at the bedside with the best medicine known to man. Yes, they should be oiled with oil and they should be prayed over. Doctors should recognize the importance of prayer and the church should support the efforts of doctors. Going to a medical doctor does not show a lack of faith. Luke himself was a medical doctor (Colossians 4:14).

The point James was making here is that the church should not just say, "I'll pray for you." The church should be in touch with a hurting world. If people are weak physically, we are to help ease the hurt. If they are weak emotionally, we are to rub in the oil of encouragement. When we ourselves are strung out, defeated and discouraged, weak and wounded, losing the battle of the spirit, we should call for the elders so that they can pray for us and encourage us.

The Prayer

The prayer must be "offered in faith" (James 5:15). Earlier James said, "When he asks, he must believe and not doubt, because he who doubts is like a wave of the sea, blown and tossed by the wind" (James 1:6). Paul stated, "Everything that does not come from faith is sin" (Romans 14:23). Jesus put it like this: "Whatever you ask for in prayer, believe that you have received it, and it will be yours" (Mark 11:24).

How do we pray in faith? Faith is found in the Word of God. Romans 10:17 says, "Faith comes from hearing the message, and the message is heard through the word of Christ." The Bible is God's personal word to you and me. It is impossible to pray in faith unless we have been alone with God and have received from Him the Word on which to stand. First John 5:14–15 says, "This is the confidence we have in approaching God: that if we ask anything according to his will, he hears us. And if we know that he hears us — whatever we ask — we know that we have what we asked of him."

Prayer must be according to God's will. I did not give my children everything for which they asked because I knew basically what was best for them. To be honest, I am extremely grateful that God has not given me everything I have asked of Him. At times, my personal prejudices and desires have taken precedence over His will for me. I have asked Him a thousand times to give me something He had no intention of giving me because He had something far better in mind. It sounds exciting and attractive to tell people, "You can have anything you ask for," but that's not Biblical. The prayer of faith is grounded in the Word that God gives to you or it is not the prayer of faith. This prayer is always offered in accordance with God's sovereign will, for all prayer is subject to His will. Remember James 4:15 says,

"You ought to say, 'If it is the Lord's will, we will live and do this or that.'" Prayer offered in faith is prayed according to God's will, and when we agree with Him, His will will be done.

The Provision

"The prayer offered in faith will make the sick person well; the Lord will raise him up. If he has sinned, he will be forgiven" (James 5:15). This verse is not a carte blanche for healing. It brings us face to face with another question: Is it God's will that everyone be healed? If so, why did Paul indicate that he "left Trophimus sick in Miletus" (2 Timothy 4:20) instead of healing him? Why did Paul allow Epaphroditus to become ill and almost die? (Philippians 2:25–27) Why did Paul ask the Lord three times to remove the thorn in his flesh, only to hear the Lord say, "My grace is sufficient for you"? (2 Corinthians 12:9) Why did Paul write to Timothy, "Use a little wine because of your stomach and your frequent illnesses"? (1 Timothy 5:23) The point is, while God can do everything and can preserve and restore any of His people from sickness, it is plainly not always His will to do so.

Physical healing is a mystery. It is wrapped up in the council of God's will. Many people think they have it all figured out, but they don't. Some people say that everyone is supposed to be well. Yet, God did not heal Paul. Other people say that sickness is the result of sin in one's life. Yet, some of God's greatest saints have lived with much pain and sickness while some of the most sinful people have been free of pain and sickness. Still, other people say that healing has to do with attitude. Yet, no one had a more pitiful attitude than Naaman. After trying to buy his cure from Elisha, he was insulted when he was told to dip in the Jordan River. He thought he was too good, but God healed him. Some people say that we have to ask for healing. Yet the crippled man at the temple gate in Acts 3 did not ask Peter to heal him. He only asked for money. We cannot put God into a box. There is no magic formula for healing. He is the Sovereign Lord.

Healing is divine. Medical doctors do not heal. Medicine does not heal. Proper diet does not heal. Exercise does not heal. God heals! He uses doctors and other means, but He is the one who brings healing. Our part is to pray and believe.

I am convinced that James had far more in mind than the physical dimension when he talked about this prayer of faith. I believe he had a spiritual uplift in mind. That's why we see this addendum to James 5:15: "If he has sinned, he will be forgiven." How easy it is to fall into sin when we are weary in well-doing. When we are too defeated to pray and our guard is down, we are so prone to sin. But according to 1 John 1:9, "If we confess our sins, he [God] is faithful and just and will forgive us our sins and purify us from all unrighteousness." James assumed his readers realized that confession is part of restoration. Only confession of sin will completely cure those sicknesses that are complicated by guilt and fear resulting from sin. And we need to confess our sins when God allows sickness and weakness in order to bring us back into fellowship with Himself.

We now understand the situation of James' readers. He was writing to those facing pressure, who were not happy. He was writing to those experiencing pleasure, who were not hurting. He was also writing to those who hurt, who were not healthy. If the church is to be in touch with a hurting world, we must be people of prayer and people of praise. We must be people who pursue holiness before God and who are not ashamed to ask elders to pray with us and for others.

II. The Solution
James 5:16

A Horizontal Solution

James 5:16 says, "Confess your sins to each other." This is the horizontal solution. James did not mean that we should go around confessing all our sins to others. We are privileged to go straight to God through the Lord Jesus Christ with our sins. However, there are times when, to be right with God, we must be right with each other. That is, to be right vertically, we must be right horizontally. When we sin against God alone, we privately ask Him to forgive us. This is private confession. Some secret sins need to be confessed only to the Lord. Psalm 90:8 says, "You [God] have set our iniquities before you, our secret sins in the light of your presence."

When we sin against another person, we must personally ask that person to forgive us. This is personal confession. Jesus said, "If you are offering your gift at the altar and there remember that your brother has something against you, leave your gift there in front of the altar. First go and be reconciled to your brother; then come and offer your gift" (Matthew 5:23–24). When we sin against a brother or sister in Christ, God puts it upon our hearts to be reconciled with that person. Personal confession can be difficult. It is hard enough for some of us to admit that we have sinned against someone, much less admit it to that person. But confessing our sins to each other prevents barriers from coming between us. There is also public confession. Sometimes when our sin has affected the entire church, we must confess it publicly.

The horizontal solution involves confession and restoration. If the church is to be in touch with a hurting world, we must carry on a ministry of restoration. Jesus said, "If your brother sins against you, go and show him his fault, just between the two of you. If he listens to you, you have won your brother over" (Matthew 18:15). Paul said, "Brothers, if someone is caught in a sin, you who are spiritual should restore him gently. But watch yourself, or you also may be tempted" (Galatians 6:1). We need to be accountable to each other as we walk along the Christian way.

A Vertical Solution

James said that we are also "to pray for each other." What a privilege it is to pray for one another. The church in touch with God on behalf of each other is the vertical solution. It is difficult to hold something against someone for whom we are sincerely praying. This is why James said that the solution must be vertical as well as horizontal.

The tense of these verbs in James 5:16 is the present imperative.[5] In other words, confession and prayer are not once-and-for-all actions as certain aorist tenses would have indicated. James was saying in effect, "Make a practice of agreeing with and praying for one another. Don't wait until the need arises. Always do it." A praying church can be in touch with a hurting world if believers know the secret of effectiveness in prayer.

III. The Secret
James 5:16–18

The Greek word translated "prayer" in James 5:16 is δέησις, which means "a humble begging or plea or petition."[6] It is the most humble word for prayer in Greek. It is not, therefore, the type of prayer that orders God to do this or that or that claims this or that. This particular word suggests a picture of a needy man with his head bowed and a dirty cap rolled in his hands. He is humbly asking for help, not demanding or claiming something that is due him. Humble prayer of the nature of δέησις is approached with integrity, asked with intensity and answered with immensity.

Approached with Integrity

James 5:16 says that δέησις is "the prayer of a righteous man." That word "righteous" is threatening. Our first reaction may be to exclaim, "That can't be me. That leaves me out." Something about that word has a forbidding ring to it. At this very point, James inserted the illustration of Elijah and reminded us that he was "a man just like us" (James 5:17). Elijah could be on the mountaintop one minute and under the juniper tree the next. He could face problems one minute and flee from them the next. He was ordinary, but he was righteous. He was right with God. James was not talking here about "supersaints," but about men and women like you and me.

Some people believe that we are all righteous in Christ because "God made him who had no sin to be sin for us, so that in him we might become the righteousness of God" (2 Corinthians 5:21). And we do stand righteous before God in the person of Christ. This is why Edward Mote said in the last verse of "The Solid Rock":

> *When He shall come with trumpet sound,*
> *Oh, may I then in Him be found:*
> *Dressed in His righteousness alone,*
> *Faultless to stand before the throne.*

However, if spiritual righteousness is at issue here, why are so many prayers unanswered? Actually, it is moral righteousness that is at issue here. James was speaking of the kind of integrity mentioned in 1 John 3:7: "Dear children, do not let anyone lead you astray. He who does what is right is righteous, just as he is righteous." Being comes before doing, but doing is always the test of our being. To get our prayers answered with immensity, they need to be approached with integrity. First John 3:22 says that we "receive from him anything we ask, because we obey his commands and do what pleases him."

If we really want to touch a hurting world, we must be men and women of integrity — righteous people who practice what we preach. Otherwise, we are "a resounding gong or a clanging cymbal" (1 Corinthians 13:1). The secret to touching our world is to pray the prayer of faith that is approached with integrity.

Asked with Intensity

"The prayer of a righteous man is powerful" (James 5:16). We derive our word "energy" from the Greek word that is translated "powerful" here. The original word literally means "stretched out" and suggests a picture of an athlete stretching for the finish line with his last gasp of energy.[7] When we strive to live in obedience to the Lord, our prayers have a persuasive energy about them. They are "powerful." The prayers that get results in the Bible are not long, drawn-out orations with lofty-sounding words. They are pointed and powerful, asked with intensity, and approached with integrity. They are prayers like the one the publican prayed: "God, have mercy on me, a sinner" (Luke 18:13). They are prayers like the one Simon Peter prayed on the sea: "Lord, save me!" (Matthew 14:30) They are prayers like Jacob's: "I will not let you go unless you bless me" (Genesis 32:26).

Many parents today need to know how to pray prayers that are approached with integrity and asked with intensity. I have basically prayed three things for our children and now, our grandchildren. I have prayed for their *path* (Psalm 16:11).

I want them to know the will of God. I have prayed for their *partners*. I believe that somewhere God is preparing the ones who will complete them. I have prayed for their *purity*. I have prayed that they might be pure in mind, that God might give them a spirit of wisdom and revelation (Ephesians 1:18). I have prayed that they might be pure in motive, that they might want to please God (1 Corinthians 10:31). I have prayed that they might be pure in morals.

All people need to know how to pray prayers that are approached with integrity and asked with intensity. James' secret is that such prayers will be answered with immensity.

Answered with Immensity

"The prayer of a righteous man is powerful and effective" (James 5:16). In the words of the King James Version, the prayer "availeth much." If we do what is right and pray in humility in a spirit of energy, God answers our prayers.

Elijah, a man like us, found the secret. He approached prayer with integrity, asked with intensity and received answers with immensity. He prayed the prayer of faith. God revealed His will and Elijah simply got in on it.

We might wonder what all of this has to do with healing. Why didn't James use as an illustration Naaman who was healed of leprosy or the Shunammite woman whose son was brought back to life? Why would James illustrate this truth using Elijah praying for rain? The reason is that James 5:13–16 primarily deals with spiritual and emotional well-being, not physical well-being. The passage has to do with a refreshing rain of Heaven falling on a dry and barren soul, bringing new life and hope.

God is in the business of divinely intervening in the natural process. Sometimes He uses doctors and medicine, but it is God who heals the sick. James 5:15 says, *"The Lord* will raise him up" *(italics added)*. God can do anything. When we pray, we pray to a God who is not limited by any cell He has ever created. God is able to answer with immensity.

A prayer that is answered with immensity is effective. Effective prayer will help us make a difference in our hurting world. We have wonderful opportunities to bring help, hope and healing to hurting, pressured people. "The prayer of a righteous man is powerful and effective" (James 5:16). God help us be His hand extended and touch a hurting world.

··
⊛ CHAPTER THIRTEEN ⊛
··

RESTORATION
JAMES 5:19-20

I. The Possibility of Our Falling (James 5:19)
II. The Responsibility of Our Calling (James 5:19-20)

A beautiful antique table graces the entrance way of our home. I acquired it at an old Oklahoma farmhouse auction in 1972. For many years before the auction, the table had been sitting out in the barn. Chickens had roosted on it, and greasy tools had lain on it. It was ugly, so no one even bid on it. I bought that weather-beaten and abused table for just a few dollars and took it to a man in Hobart who loved to restore old furniture. He stripped that table down and restored its beauty. Today, it is one of our most cherished possessions.

God is in the restoration business, too. And the remarkable thing about it is that He uses us as believers to help bring restoration to people who have been placed in the barn, beaten up by life's circumstances, knocked around and finally put over to the side when they were no longer beautiful.

James closes his letter with the recurring theme of the second chance. He reminded us of the possibility of our falling. Just because we are followers of Christ does not mean we cannot "wander from the truth" (James 5:19). Paul said, "If you think you are standing firm, be careful that you don't fall!" (1 Corinthians 10:12). James also reminded us of the responsibility of our calling. As members of God's forever family, we have responsibilities to each other. We have a ministry of reconciliation — the restoration of fallen believers.

I. The Possibility of Our Falling
James 5:19

James called on us to note the person, the path and the place of our falling.

The Person Is a Disciple

James was addressing his "brothers" (James 5:19). The Greek word for "brother," ἀδελφός, occurs 19 times in James' Epistle. It means "one who shares with another a mutual life." My wife, Susie, and I have two daughters, Wendy and Holly. They have the same parents. They share our life. Our blood courses through their veins. Likewise, we are born into God's family and share His life. We have trusted in Christ and, consequently, He is alive in us. We are God's children, and we have a mutually shared life with our brothers and sisters — the life of Christ. We have a special relationship with each other. We are more closely related to each other through the blood of Christ than we are to our own unsaved blood relatives who have never put their faith and trust in Him.

James 5:19 is talking about a believer, "one of you." He is not talking about a lost person. The point is that it is possible for a true believer to leave the path. This does not mean that a fallen brother is no longer a Christian. One who has been born into Christ's family can never sever that relationship. Jesus likens spiritual birth to physical birth. It only takes place once. If your physical child disobeys you, does not speak to you for a week or never thanks you for gifts, does that mean the relationship is broken? Does that mean he is no longer your child? No. He has been born into your family, and although the fellowship may be damaged, the relationship cannot be severed. There is a great difference between relationship and fellowship. James was saying that the believer's fellowship within the family of God can be damaged, but the good news is that it can be restored.

James introduced his thought about falling with an important word: "if." The use of this word means that James was not referring to an actual instance in the past, but to a "probable one in the future."[1] This "if" is like a flashing yellow light saying, "Caution, caution, caution!" It is not a red light. Just because there is potential danger ahead, we should not stop our normal lives and isolate ourselves from the world. Some Christians do this, but isolation is foreign to New Testament teaching. We are to be the salt of the earth and the light of the world. We are to penetrate a lost society. Remember, Jesus not only grew in favor with God but also in favor with man.

Life has many intersections. James was saying that when we approach them, we must remember the "if" — the flashing yellow light. We must look both ways, for there is potential danger. We could get sideswiped or make a wrong turn. We must be cautious so that we won't make a wrong turn or have a wreck.

The Path Is Deceptive

James 5:19 says that it is possible to "wander from the truth." "Wander" is a translation of the Greek word πλανάω, which means "to go astray." This word suggests a gradual moving away from the will of God. Jesus uses this same word in Matthew 18:12: "If a man owns a hundred sheep, and one of them wanders away, will he not leave the ninety-nine on the hills and go to look for the one that wandered off?" How did the sheep wander away? It didn't intend to do that. There was a little patch of grass here, so the sheep kept his head down and followed his appetite. Then it wandered to the next patch of grass, and the next, and before the little sheep knew it, it had wandered away.

There is a danger of wandering away in the life of a Christian. Peter used πλανάω when he said, "You were like sheep going astray, but now you have returned to the Shepherd and Overseer of your souls" (1 Peter 2:25). Wandering happens subtly. The path is deceptive.

This verb, πλανάω, is in the aorist tense, indicating that the wandering is not habitual, but a one-time or occasional slip. The action was completed in the past; the believer is not repeating it over and over again. (When a particular sin is habitual, it is a good indication that the individual has never been truly saved.) Interestingly, the verb πλανάω is in the passive voice, indicating that wandering believers are led astray by some outside force — perhaps a person, a place or a passion.

Matthew 24:4 uses πλανάω when it warns, "Watch out that no one *deceives* you" *(italics added)*. We must be careful. The path is deceptive. We do not just plunge headlong into sin; we wander into it a step at a time. Perhaps we leave the Bible closed or forget to pray. Maybe we begin to spend time with new friends who are not believers and go to new places. A step here, a step there, and then we fall!

The Place Is Doctrinal

James 5:19 says that we can go astray "from the truth." This is vitally important to note. Jesus Christ says He is "the truth" (John 14:6). John said, "Sanctify them by the truth; your word is truth" (17:17). "Truth" refers to the Living Word and to the written Word. The same Greek word, ἀλήθεια, is translated "truth" in both John 14:6 and 17:17. Using this same term, James was saying, "Don't wander away from the Word." We must not put our convictions on the shelf. If we do not stay close to the truth, we will wander away from it.

Today more and more people say that doctrine does not matter. However, what we believe determines how we behave. If we believe that we are no different from animals — that indeed we evolved from monkeys — we will begin to act like animals. On the other hand, if we believe that we are special creations of God, that He formed us and fashioned us and called us by name before we were born, we will act like human beings made in His image. If we believe that we are here for a purpose and not by some chance of science, and we are different from all other species because we have a spirit by which we can connect with God, that belief will affect our behavior. Don't let anyone ever tell you that what you believe doesn't matter. Belief determines behavior.

It is possible for a believer to wander away from the place of sound doctrine or truth. When one of us wanders away from doctrine, he eventually wanders from duty. When one wanders from belief, his behavior soon follows. When one wanders from the Word, his walk will wander, also.

II. The Responsibility of Our Calling
James 5:19–20

The Greek word for "church," ἐκκλησία, is found 115 times in the New Testament and literally means "the called-out ones." With our calling comes a responsibility to Christ, to the church and to each other. We have the responsibility to bring back fellow believers who have fallen — to bring them to repentance, resuscitation and restoration. Paul said that Christ "gave us the ministry of reconciliation" (2 Corinthians 5:18). He also admonished, "If someone is caught in a sin, you who are spiritual should restore him gently" (Galatians 6:1). James said, "Someone should bring him back" (James 5:19). This is the responsibility of our calling.

What is your first reaction when you hear that someone in the faith has fallen? Do you rush to the telephone and say, "Did you hear?" Do you delight in spreading the news? Do you point the finger of accusation or condemnation? Do you wring your hands in anticipation of excommunication? Or are you burdened enough to want to go and help bring that person back?

In our zeal to win the lost, we sometimes forget we are also to win the saved. We have the responsibility according to James 5:19–20 to "bring them back" (repentance), "save them from death" (resuscitation) and "cover over a multitude of sins" (restoration).

A Call to Repentance

How wonderful it is to know we can come back and start all over again. This is good news. Even though we may have fallen and wandered from the truth, we do not have to stay on the path of deception. We can realize our mistakes, return to the intersection where we made the wrong turn and start over again.

The Greek word translated "bring back," ἐπιστρέφω, literally means "to turn around, to turn back." The same word is found in Luke 22:32: Jesus said to Simon Peter, "I have prayed for you, Simon, that your faith may not fail. And when you have turned back, strengthen your brothers." After Peter repented, he resumed the responsibility of his calling.

James was writing to those who knew what it is to walk on the right path and was exhorting them to turn back to it. James was not talking about someone who is sorry he got caught. He was not talking about someone who starts over, but then makes the wrong turn again and continues to commit a particular sin. That is not restoration. James was talking about men and women who really come back, who turn from the error of their way

(James 5:20). Repentance is the key to restoration. We cannot make someone turn back. Our responsibility is to confront the wanderer in love and seek to bring him back. I have done this many times. Some have come back, while others have remained on their wandering pathway.

Some people say when a person wanders from the truth, he loses his salvation. But haven't all of us sinned sometime along the way? There were times when we knew the Bible said to do a certain thing, but we didn't do it. We knew we should read the Bible, but for awhile we didn't even open the Book. And what about all the sins of omission? If every time we wandered from the path we lost our salvation, some of us would be gaining it and losing it hourly. Salvation would be a game of chance. There is no victory in that. There is no peace in that. There is no assurance in that. Jesus did not go to the cross for us to live that way. He died for our past sins (Titus 3:5). He died for our present sins (1 Corinthians 15:1–2). He died for our future sins (Romans 5:9). If your salvation is only in the past, it is not authentic.

Some people have the security of the believer confused with the security of the church member. Many people on church rolls are not saved. About them Jesus says, "Many will say to me on that day, 'Lord, Lord...' Then I will tell them plainly, 'I never knew you'" (Matthew 7:22–23).

There is a difference between the sin of a non-believer and the sin of a believer. A non-believer habitually sins, committing the same sin over and over, with no conviction of wrong. A believer cannot do that. He may wander, but he will not do so habitually. A true believer will be convicted in his heart to come back. The responsibility of our calling is to encourage him to come to repentance, to begin again.

A Call to Resuscitation

James 5:20 says, "Whoever turns a sinner from the error of his way will save him from death." The Greek word translated "death" here is θάνατος, which in a sense could be translated "punishment."[2] Eternal death is not at issue here. The word James uses here refers to physical death. James was referring here to the "sin unto death" mentioned in 1 John 5:16–17: "If anyone sees his brother commit a sin that does not lead to death, he should pray and God will give him life. I refer to those whose sin does not lead to death. There is a sin that leads to death. I am not saying that he should pray about that. All wrongdoing is sin, and there is sin that does not lead to death." When a Christian becomes rebellious and unrepentant, sometimes God takes him out prematurely through physical death. Thus, when we bring our brothers and sisters back to God, sometimes we save them from death.

Ananias and Sapphira sinned unto death (Acts 5). Did God strike them down to get even? No, God mercifully dismissed Ananias and Sapphira from earth in order to keep them from further sin. In a sense, I think God said, "Come on home if you're going to act that way."

Because Moses sinned by perverting the type of Christ and striking the rock rather than speaking to it, he did not get to lead his people into the promised land (Numbers 20; Deuteronomy 34). Instead, he died on Mount Nebo and God buried him. There is a sin unto death.

When Christians fall out of the will of God and refuse to repent, God may chasten them — sometimes even with death. But we are not to judge them, for only God knows the motives of their hearts. "The Lord does not look at the things man looks at. Man looks at the outward appearance, but the Lord looks at the heart" (1 Samuel 16:7).

God will not allow the sin of believers to go unchecked. Paul wrote about this very point: "Hand this man over to Satan, so that the sinful nature may be destroyed and his spirit saved on the day of the Lord" (1 Corinthians 5:5). It is a fearful thing to fall into the hands of the holy God. That's what happened to some of the Corinthian believers who were scandalously abusing the Lord's supper and getting drunk while observing it. Suddenly, they were becoming ill and dying prematurely for no apparent reason. Paul warned them about their actions: "That is why many among you are weak and sick, and a number of you have fallen asleep" (1 Corinthians 11:30).

Responsibility goes with our calling. We are to bring our fellow believers back, save them from death and help them start over.

A Call to Restoration

James 5:20 says, "Whoever turns a sinner from the error of his way will save him from death and cover over a multitude of sins." The Greek word translated "cover over," καλύπτω, means "to hide or veil." Καλύπτω is used eight times in the New Testament. In Matthew 8:24, it describes how the waves swept over the boat. In Luke 8:16, it conveys a picture of a lamp hidden in a jar. Peter used the word when he said, "Above all, love each other deeply, because love covers over a multitude of sins" (1 Peter 4:8).

A person who repents and returns to the Lord has his sins covered. The only way to cover sin is through the atonement of Christ. Sin is only covered through God's substitutionary sacrifice for sin in the blood of Jesus Christ. David wrote, "Blessed is he whose transgressions are forgiven, whose sins are covered" (Psalm 32:1). When a Christian repents and comes back, his sins can no longer be seen. They have been removed "as far as the east is from the west" (Psalm 103:12) and God remembers them no more. It doesn't really matter how many sins he has, even if it is a multitude. They can be taken away and covered by the blood of Jesus Christ. This is why we sing:

Calvary covers it all,
My past with its sin and stain;
My guilt and despair Jesus took on Him there,
And Calvary covers it all.[3]

Note that in Psalm 51:12 David pled, "Restore to me the joy of your salvation." He did not ask for his salvation to be restored because he never lost it. He had lost his joy. He had lost the thrill of walking each day with his Maker. The Christian who has lost his joy can have his joy restored when his sins are covered over.

It's wonderful to realize that God calls on us to be His agents in proclaiming this glorious good news. This is what the church should be about — the ministry of reconciliation. The responsibility that comes with our calling is to bring others to repentance, resuscitation and restoration. And we are to carry out our responsibility in love. Solomon said, "Hatred stirs up dissension, but love covers over all wrongs" (Proverbs 10:12).

We should not misunderstand this truth. Love does not sweep the dirt under the carpet. Where there is true love, there is also truth. Paul said we are to speak the truth in love (Ephesians 4:15). Some people speak the truth, but don't do it in love. They are judgmental, condemning and critical. Others speak in love, but do not speak the truth. They are so concerned about speaking softly and nicely that they wander from the truth of God's Word. We are to speak the truth in love in such a way that we will bring the wanderer home.

We should remember an important twofold principle. First, everything we cover God will uncover. Paul said: "Therefore judge nothing before the appointed time; wait till the Lord comes. He will bring to light what is hidden in darkness and will expose the motives of men's hearts. At that time each will receive his praise from God" (1 Corinthians 4:5). Second, everything we uncover God will cover. Solomon said, "He who conceals his sin does not prosper, but whoever confesses and renounces them finds mercy" (Proverbs 28:13). Jesus said, "Whatever is hidden is meant to be disclosed, and whatever is concealed is meant to be brought out into the open" (Mark 4:22).

Every time I walk in the front door of my home and see that restored table in the hallway, I am reminded that the Lord Jesus Christ is in the restoration business. So many among us are battered and bruised like that old table used to be. They have been stuck in back corners and have lost their beauty. Let's take them by the hand and bring them to the One who can make old things pass away and all things become new. Let's answer God's call to be His agents in restoration.

With this call stated succinctly in James 5:19–20, the letter rather abruptly ends. This ending is quite a contrast to the way Paul concluded his letters. For example, he closed the second Corinthian letter with these words: "Finally, brothers, good-by. Aim for perfection, listen to my appeal, be of one mind, live in peace. And the God of love and peace will be with you. Greet one another with a holy kiss. All the saints send their greetings. May the grace of the Lord Jesus Christ, and the love of God, and the fellowship of the Holy Spirit be with you all" (2 Corinthians 13:11–14). James' ending is also in considerable contrast to the way Peter concluded his letters: "But grow in the grace and knowledge of our Lord and Savior Jesus Christ. To him be glory both now and forever! Amen" (2 Peter 3:18). Jude closed by saying, "To him who is able to keep you from falling and to present you before his glorious presence without fault and with great joy — to the only God our Savior be glory, majesty, power and authority, through Jesus Christ our Lord, before all ages, now and forevermore! Amen" (Jude 24–25). The apostle John concluded his third letter by saying: "I have much to write you, but I do not want to do so with pen and ink. I hope to see you soon, and we will talk face to face. Peace to you. The friends here send their greetings. Greet the friends there by name" (3 John 13–14).

James concluded his Epistle rather abruptly because he was a practical man. He told us what we are to do and then said in effect, "Now get on with it."

As the customer in the fabric store said, "It is time to get down to brass tacks."

❀ NOTES ❀

Chapter 1

1. John Blanchard, *Not Hearers Only*, Vol. 1 (London: Word, 1971) 42.

2. George Sweeting, *How to Solve Conflicts* (Chicago: Moody Bible Institute, 1973) 13.

Chapter 2

1. George Harris, *Hallelujah We Believe* (Nashville: Nelson, 1986) 25.

2. Spiros Zodhiates, *The Work of Faith* (Chattanooga: AMG, 1981) 69.

3. G. Campbell Morgan, *The Westminster Pulpit* (Westwood, NJ: Revell, 1954) 72.

4. A. T. Robertson, *Word Pictures in the New Testament* (Nashville: Broadman, 1933) 18.

5   Zodhiates, *Work of Faith*, 72.

6. Ethel Barrett, *Will the Real Phony Please Stand Up?* (Glendale, CA. Regal, 1969) 32.

7. Thomas O. Chisholm, "Great Is Thy Faithfulness" (Carol Stream, IL: Hope, 1923).

Chapter 3

1   Zodhiates, *Work of Faith*, 105.

2. Fritz Rienecker, *A Linguistic Key to the Greek New Testament* (Grand Rapids: Zondervan, 1976) 726.

3. R. C. Lenski, *The Interpretation of the Epistle to the Hebrews and the Epistle of James* (Minneapolis: Augsburg, 1966) 522.

4. Zodhiates, *Work of Faith*, 134.

5. Robertson, *Word Pictures*, 25.

6. Zodhiates, *Work of Faith*, 143.

Chapter 4

1. Sweeting, *How to Solve Conflicts*, 53.
2. *Life Application Bible* (Wheaton, IL: Tyndale, 1986) 604.
3. Blanchard, *Not Hearers Only*, Vol. 2, 22.
4. Zodhiates, *Work of Faith*, 162.
5. Ibid., 184.
6. Ibid., 193.

Chapter 5

1. Rienecker, *Linguistic Key*, 730.
2. Douglas J. Moo, *Tyndale New Testament Commentaries* (Leicester, England: InterVarsity Press, 1985) 101.
3. Roy B. Zuck, *The Bible Knowledge Commentary*, Vol. N. T. (Wheaton, IL: Victor, 1983) 836.
4. Zodhiates, *The Labor of Love* (Chattanooga: AMG, 1981) 29.
5. Rienecker, *Linguistic Key*, 730.
6. Moo, *Tyndale Commentaries*, 107.
7. Rienecker, *Linguistic Key*, 732.
8. Zuck, *Bible Knowledge Commentary*, 826.
9. Sweeting, *How to Solve Conflicts*, 70.

Chapter 6

1. Ibid., 74.
2. Zodhiates, *Labor of Love*, 94.
3. Warren W. Wiersbe, *The Bible Exposition Commentary*, Vol. 2 (Wheaton, IL: Victor, 1989) 360.

Chapter 7

1. Moo, *Tyndale Commentaries*, 134.

2. Robertson, *Word Pictures*, 46.

3. Wiersbe, *Bible Exposition Commentary*, 364.

4. Zodhiates, *Labor of Love*, 153.

5. William Barclay, *The Letters of James and Peter* (Louisville: Westminster, 1958) 107.

6. Rienecker, *Linguistic Key*, 735.

7. Ibid., 735.

8. Moo, *Tyndale Commentaries*, 135.

Chapter 8

1. Blanchard, *Not Hearers Only*, Vol. 3, 16.

2. Wiersbe, *Bible Exposition Commentary*, 368.

3. Zodhiates, *Labor of Love*, 237.

Chapter 9

1. O. S. Hawkins, *Jonah* (Neptune, NJ: Loizeaux, 1990) 32–33.

2. Wiersbe, *Bible Exposition Commentary*, 371.

3. Gloria and William J. Gaither, "Because He Lives," © copyright 1971 by William J. Gaither, all rights reserved, used by permission of Gaither Music Company.

4. Zodhiates, *The Patience of Hope* (Chattanooga: AMG, 1981) 34.

Chapter 10

1. Zuck, *Bible Knowledge Commentary*, 832.
2. Moo, *Tyndale Commentaries*, 163.
3. Lenski, *Interpretation*, 650.
4. James T. Draper, *James: Faith and Works in Balance* (Wheaton, IL: Tyndale, 1981) 147.
5. Zodhiates, *Patience of Hope*, 56.
6. Moo, *Tyndale Commentaries*, 161.
7. Zodhiates, *Patience of Hope*, 47.
8. Ibid., 53.
9. Wiersbe, *Bible Exposition Commentary*, 337.
10. Alec Motyer, *The Message of James* (Leicester, England: InterVarsity Press, 1985) 167.
11. Zuck, *Bible Knowledge Commentary*, 833.
12. Rienecker, *Linguistic Key*, 740.

Chapter 11

1. Blanchard, *Not Hearers Only*, Vol. 4, 38.
2. Zodhiates, *Patience of Hope*, 89.
3. Ibid., 93.

Chapter 12

1. Ibid., 115.
2. Robert G. Witty, *Divine Healing* (Nashville: Broadman, 1989) 186.
3. Rienecker, *Linguistic Key*, 741.
4. Ibid.
5. Lenski, *Interpretation*, 666.
6. Ibid., 667.
7. Blanchard, *Not Hearers Only*, Vol. 4, 83.

Chapter 13

1. Zodhiates, *Patience of Hope*, 215.

2. Ibid., 232.

3. Mrs. Walter G. Taylor, "Calvary Covers It All" (Irving, TX: Rodeheaver, 1934).

⊛ ABOUT GUIDESTONE FINANCIAL RESOURCES ⊛

GuideStone®
Financial Resources

Dallas-based GuideStone Financial Resources is a leading financial services provider of retirement, investment and life and health plans. Operating as a church benefits board, the multi-billion-dollar organization is dedicated to providing outstanding products and high-touch customer service to Southern Baptist and other evangelical churches, ministries and institutions.

GuideStone offers a wide array of retirement services including retirement and executive compensation plans, personal and institutional investment products and record-keeping services. Christian-based, socially screened investment programs utilize a sophisticated manager-of-managers philosophy.

Life and Health products made available through GuideStone include a variety of term life, accident, disability, medical and dental plans with a wide range of benefit options.

GuideStone's insurance agency affiliate, GuideStone Agency Services, makes available full lines of property and casualty coverage as well as risk management education and tools designed with the ministry in mind.

Founded in 1918 as a relief organization, GuideStone continues its tradition of providing financial assistance to retired Southern Baptist ministers and ministers' widows with insufficient retirement income through its Mission:Dignity program. For more information about GuideStone's products, services and endowment opportunities, visit *www.GuideStone.org* or call toll-free at **1-888-98-GUIDE** (1-888-984-8433).